M000278191

"*All In* shares powerful stories from Allen's own journey to help answer many of the questions and issues leaders face in both their professional and personal lives."

Joe Gibbs, Pro Football and NASCAR Hall of Fame

"*All In* is a priceless resource for men who are brave enough to take a deep look at what is most essential in life. Allen Morris's brave and personal storytelling models the path 'men on a mission' need to move from doing good to being great. If you want to die with no regrets ... read and live this book."

Tom Daly, PhD, Mentor, Leadership Trainer, 4 Gateways Coaching

"One of the most admirable as well as powerful traits of a great leader is the courage to be vulnerable and authentic with ourselves and others. Allen graciously and openly shares his own journey of healing in his newest book *All In*. We owe it to ourselves and especially to our families, our teams, and those in our spheres of influence to take ourselves off autopilot and relentlessly pursue a life that is ALL IN. It is a choice that we all have the freedom and privilege to make, and Allen's story provides deep insights into how each of us can reach our best selves and the life God purposed for us from the beginning."

Lisa Nichols, CEO, Technology Partners

"A man who seemingly had everything in life discusses his personal journey of pain, faith, relationships, and the true meaning of success. Allen Morris's story is a profile in courage and inspiration."

Erik Bethel, former US Director of the World Bank

"I could not put it down and read half the book in two afternoons. So much of what Allen speaks about touches me at my core."

Mitchell D. Brandt, CEO, Blue Jay Academy

"*All In* is an extremely powerful life story. The journey of self-discovery and the transformation of adversity make this book a fascinating read. It is inspirational to know that you can turn danger into growth and success. Every moment of our lives becomes a teachable moment. Those who can identify them will change the outcome of their own destiny."
Diego Perez, Tae Kwon Do Grandmaster

"Much like the visionary building projects for which he's known, Allen Morris's *All In* is true to form—another thoughtfully assembled masterpiece. Morris peels back the vulnerability onion as he takes readers inside the hearts and minds of perfectly imperfect leaders. We're reminded that self-imposed limitations are real in all men. But they're never the final outcome for those willing to go ALL IN!"
Scott Kuehl, Founder of BrandResolve Coaching

"*All In* is a courageous introspective that will help leaders in their quest for personal improvement and true success. Not everyone will commit to the journey, but everyone will benefit from the generous identification of unspoken self-truths. Allen, thanks for showing us that we're not alone in our 'shadow.'"
Adolfo Henriques, Vice Chairman, The Related Group

"Allen Morris has taken some huge hits in his life, professionally and personally. If you ask him if he's over them, he might tell you, 'They are the X on my Treasure Map,' and that he is still mining the gold in the midst of his growth. Fortunately for the rest of us, Allen isn't keeping the treasure or the map to himself. This book is a candid and transparent reflection on his continuing growth journey, a journey I have been privileged to share as part of my own. I heartily recommend *All In* to anyone longing for a deeper reality and a richer experience of life than the thin and hollow fruit that human drivenness serves up."

Dr. Bill White, Senior Pastor, Christ Journey Church, Coral Gables, Florida

"I can wholeheartedly endorse *All In*. I so admire how transparent Allen is in sharing the story. I really believe that this book will help many men and, in essence, help change the world."

T. Dallas Smith, President and CEO, T. Dallas Smith & Company

"What are you willing to give in order to experience the life that your heart really longs for? Allen Morris's *All In* is an invitation to the most wild and dangerous adventure that a man could ever embark on. One that will put his strength and courage to the test, that will reveal his greatest weaknesses, but that will ultimately lead him to discover who he really is and experience the life that he was always created to live."

Pablo Ceron, Founder and President, WILDSONS

"*All In* packs a steady punch of powerful messages and articulately prompts self-reflection along the way. One such theme is the concept of 'human doing vs. human being' and stops the reader in his tracks to ponder our own actions and purpose. Allen intentionally compels his readers to think at the conclusion of each chapter with a 'pause and reflect' section to allow the gravity of his words to soak in and to allow our own minds creative contemplation. *All In* is a candid journey of self-help from a man who shares the gift of his experiences, insight, and perspective."
Ben Mollere, Corporate Vice President,
Baptist Health South Florida

"This is not your typical book on how to succeed in business. Instead, Allen pulls back the curtain on living the American Dream and honestly shares his experiences on finding what it takes to create a life awake."
Dr. Gary Rupp, PhD in Clinical Psychology

"I felt like a witness on an authentic journey experiencing the raw and wild twists and turns of Allen's transformation. On a second read, I shifted seats—from passive witness to active player—and understood that the book, its story and message, is a how-to guide for me (and us) to become ALL IN every day."
Barry Kaplan, Executive Coach and Author of
The Power of Vulnerability: How to Create a Team of Leaders
by Shifting INward

"Allen has written, using his own painful and ongoing victorious journey, a manual for those daring shared vulnerability toward wholeness in a safe container called Forum. His key to reclaiming personal healing and passion for one's mission in life. All-en is ALL IN."
Rev. Dr. Carlos M. Salabarria

"This is the type of book that makes you understand more about yourself and about life. A masterfully written account of personal success, failure, confusion, trauma, and pain. Modeling courage and humility while skillfully learning vulnerability and grace, Allen leads us through his journey to physical, emotional, and spiritual healing. An inspiring must-read for all leaders!"
Debbie Holcomb, Certified Shadow Work Leader,
Coach, Facilitator, Trainer Gracing Experience,
Cofounder of Women Revealed Weekend Retreats

"Allen takes us on a powerful journey of looking at the deeper parts of ourselves that impact our lives in a meaningful way. He provides insights and tools you can use to support you on your journey. A must-read!"
John Drury, YPO Facilitator and Author of
Awaken Your Soul: A Journey of Discovery

"Allen Morris has crafted a provocative message through the substance of his decades of experiences. Saturated with self-disclosure and honed as a genuine step-by-step on-ramp into transformation, *All In* is an authentic and daring invitation for the leader within every soul."
Morgan Snyder, Author of *Becoming a King*, Founder,
BecomeGoodSoil.com, Vice President, Wild at Heart

"Allen has been humbly sharing his journey and inpacting my life well before he wrote this book. In this book, he gives an unvarnished, humorous look both of the highs and lows of his remarkable life in a frank and approachable way. I hope that others glean the insights and benefit from hearing about Allen's journey as I have."
Raul Segredo, CEO, Avionica

"As head of one of the country's largest boys' schools, I see high-achieving boys on a path to success and leadership, yet beneath the grades and wins is often an emptiness from a hole they hide and cannot fill . . . and one they may carry with them their whole lives. Full of vulnerability, Biblical wisdom, and practical steps, *All In* provides a map for men to lean into struggles, setbacks, and sorrows as they journey toward authentic manhood with purpose, integrity, and joy. Read this book if you want to pursue a deeper and more fulfilling manhood."
Lee Burns, Head of School, The McCallie School

"Allen has always been ALL IN in his journey through life. I have laughed "with," "at," "because of," and "in connection with" Allen because he is so unique, fun, transparent, and genuine. I don't know anyone who could or would write a book like this except Allen Morris!"
Harrison Merrill, Chairman & CEO, The Merrill Trust

"Allen's vulnerable sharing of his life's journey provides us a pathway for healing from pain and how a man finds himself."
Mike Pappas, CEO, The Keyes Company

"If I had to pick one word that describes the overall theme of his book, it would be 'hope.' I think we can all identify with one of more of the troublesome feelings or past experiences that Allen expresses in the pages he's written. The hope lies in the guidance he offers of how to respond to those nagging feelings!"
Ron Shuffield, President, Berkshire Hathaway HomeServices, EWM Realty

"I am gaining so much from *All In*! My eyes are being open to important new concepts. Thank you so much for taking the time to write this transformational book for leaders!

"This book will transform many lives by opening up the doors to great personal growth for many leaders who would have stayed in their current sub-optimal state for the rest of their lives."
Chris Crane, Chairman and Cofounder of edify.org

"*All In* offers effective guidance to find a positive, productive future through the help of support groups bound together by mutual trust, brotherhood, confidentiality, and faith in God. The compassionate, healing tone of his narrative relating his own life's story of worldly success crippled by the pain and suffering of human error is compelling."
Don Slesnick, Former Mayor, City of Coral Gables, Florida

"Allen's book is a masterpiece of providing insight to the ups and downs and emotional issues that confront all of us but particularly those who have demanding leadership roles. He openly shares the struggle to balance all the requirements that were placed on him as a business leader, husband, and father. Allen's book clearly demonstrates that life is a long short road! Well done."
Charles Papy III, Duane Morris, LLC

"*All In* helps make sense of the journey so many men find themselves on in life when they wonder why they have hit a wall and want to know what to do next. This much-needed resource provides a roadmap for healing and redemption, and it is illustrated by someone who has been there and experienced it.

"It's rare to find a resource that meets men where they are, dissects the challenges they face, and charts a journey toward redemption. I look forward to sharing *All In* with men looking for a lifeline during the storm in their lives and walking with them as they apply the message."
Worth Carson, Senior Pastor, Granada Church

"As an individual who fully embraces the precepts noted in Allen's book *All In*, I want to encourage everyone to read it (specifically men, because we are *horrible* at dealing with our deepest feelings) in order to help better their emotional well-being. Bad things happen, but they do not have to own us. We do have to deal with those emotions, though, as they simply do not go away. The book shares insights to begin the process of true emotional wellness, and I'm confident that everyone will find it to be a breath of fresh air."
Israel Kreps, CEO, Kreps PR & Marketing

"In his latest book *All In*, W. Allen Morris takes us through his heroic yet humbling physical, emotional, and spiritual journey. His insight to the discovery of his shadows or past pain being the key to his current peace and future growth is inspirational. The information in this book and my participation with the ALL IN retreats have helped me reconcile with my personal struggles and reach levels of joy and self-awareness I never knew [before]. We can all relate to Allen's experiences and how we will learn 'One man's work is every man's work.' No doubt this is a must-read for men, women, parents, and people in all stages of life. You will find that the human condition is one we all share, and that it's never too late to have a happy childhood."
Michael Cabanas, Regional Managing Director, Fiduciary Trust

"Allen Morris has given us a gift in *All In*. His vulnerability and life lessons learned are for anyone wanting to be truly authentic to themselves, others, and to God. I truly believe this book will give courage and freedom to many."
Debra Petersen, CRU Women's Resources,
former Radio Host and Emcee for Women of Faith

"It's amazing how Allen opens up and is vulnerable to the reader throughout the book. As a result, you're able to get invaluable insight and learn from the many life lessons and struggles that Allen has endured. You'll walk away a better man, father, and husband."
Jim Mueller, Managing Partner,
Verner Brumley Mueller Parker

"What a privilege to recommend *All In* by Allen Morris. The concepts in this book have helped change me and my marriage of fify-two years. I am a better man, husband, father, grandfather, minister, and friend as a result of applying the life principles found in this book. I recommend you read and apply it with others, not just by yourself."
Dr. Danny Levi, Retired Minister,
Presbyterian Church of America

"Wow. What a powerful and compelling narrative shared by Allen Morris in his book *All In*. As a business leader and entrepreneur, the concept of risk is familiar but it is limited to a sphere of influence that I control. I am now challenged to risk more in areas that I do not control so that I can have a greater reliance on God.

"We all want more than this world can provide; that breakthrough experience that Allen so poignantly illustrates by sharing his journey. No matter where you are at in your journey, you can go deeper in your purpose by reading—and going—ALL IN."
Gar Liebler, Visionary, Equity Experts

"I found Allen Morris's book *All In* to be refreshingly honest and extremely well written. Once I started the book, I could not put it down. Reading about the personal experiences of Allen and others made the points not only understandable, but tangible."
Anthony Barbar, Former Board Chair,
Florida Atlantic University

"In this remarkably personal account, Allen Morris reveals a life once mired in the shadow of life, but [which is] now in the joy of bringing together others motivated by a powerful intention to live wholeheartedly."
Fred Smith, Founder, The Gathering

"Allen has an incredible life story of rising quickly to success and prominence. Few leaders will as transparently share the joy, challenges, and wounds in all of life to grow and be 'ALL IN'. Allen includes learnings from deep self-awareness and practical challenges for all of us who seek something more!"
John H. Kramer, Jr., Chairman and CEO,
Cambridge Air Solutions

"Mr. Morris's book is a life-changer. You will not learn these life lessons in a classroom. I highly recommend this book and its teaching to those longing for a richer life."
Scott Sime, Sime Realty Corporation

"In this engaging memoir, Allen Morris shares how the power of authentic relationships helped him conquer personal and professional challenges and achieve even greater success than he once thought possible. If you feel stuck or unfulfilled, this practical approach can help you rediscover your passion, purpose, and joy for life."
Frank Bell, Founder, InspireCIO Leadership Network

"*All In* is a straightforward and groundbreaking challenge to men. Many of us live two lives. The outward appearance of success and accomplishment and our private worlds that many times include loneliness and despair. *All In* gives us the road map. Allen has pierced this dilemma of duplicity through his transparency of mistakes and heartaches that we can all relate to in some way or another."
Christopher White, Vice Chairman, Director,
Southeast Region Lead, Savills

"As the son of a father and mother who were respected elected officials and community leaders, I experienced many of the same pressures and wounds that Allen describes so honestly in his book *All In*. The value of his journey of self-discovery exhibits itself with great clarity, and his story inspires the reader to embark on his or her own quest to bring light into the shadows. The book reminds us that this kind of learning process is never-ending and that every day is a new opportunity for redemption and healing. I am grateful to Allen for capturing and sharing these lessons and reminders."
James Langford, President, Etowah Museum

"There's a lot more to health than not being sick. That's the truth! We all have shadow areas in our lives. Want to get healthy? Here's the key: you will only love others to the degree you love yourself, and you will only love yourself to the degree you know how much God loves you. Life is too short to get it wrong. Why not get it right? Thanks, Allen, for being real and ALL IN!"
Dr. John Tolson, Founder of the Tolson Group and
Former Team Chaplain, Houston Rockets, Houston
Oilers, Orlando Magic, and Dallas Cowboys

"We live in an age where honesty and transparency are rare, especially in leadership and areas of influence. There is an old saying that 'success builds walls and failure builds bridges.' Allen boldly invites us into a journey that gives us permission to be honest and authentic with our own lives, building those necessary bridges that are needed to be an effective and sought-after person. I hope you will be encouraged to by his example as you set course to living your compelling life."

Stephan Tchividjian, Cofounder and President,
National Christian Foundation of South Florida

"In *All In*, Allen Morris adeptly narrates his own journey of self-discovery. He sheds light on the shadow life that is a source of personal and relational dysfunction. Allen's writing is insightful, fast-paced, and engaging. The best part is that anyone can read *All In* and recognize, maybe for the first time, their own shadow life, something that anyone twenty years of age or older certainly has. Anyone can benefit by reading *All In*."

Willem H. Erwich, JD, CPWA©, SVP, Wealth Management

"As Allen Morris movingly and vulnerably shares his own life story, he raises questions and issues that many people prefer to bury. His inspirational and informative account of how he sought help, and now seeks to help many others, will be a blessing to each and every reader."

Michael Ramsden, President, RZIM

"Having known Allen for two decades, I see how he can be a source of inspiration and healing."

Mike Fernandez, Chairman, MBF Partners

"I must tell you that I found *All In* to be unique and introspective. I learned a lot about Allen and, also, myself, for which this book is intended, I believe. Thank you for reaching out through your readership to assist and assuage many inward harsh thoughts toward others that many people harbor for past 'wrongs' to show grace and fellowship to others. I liked your book very much."
Honorable Dorothy Thomson, Former Commissioner and Mayor, Coral Gables, Florida

"I have known Allen Morris longer than any other woman on earth. As his oldest sister, I can say he tells the truth about the things he wishes had gone differently in his life. His life change from those difficult years is extraordinary. Allen's stories reflect his commitment to continued personal growth in every season of life. I appreciate learning new perspectives about healthy relationships and in this book, there were many. Something he doesn't say is that he is an exceedingly generous, kind, and loving guy. I love you."
Ida Morris Bell, sister, wife, mother, grandmother

all in

w. allen morris

how to risk
everything
for everything
that matters

Forefront
BOOKS

All In
How to Risk Everything for Everything that Matters

© 2022 W. Allen Morris

All rights reserved.

No part of this book shall be reproduced or transmitted in any form
or by any means, electronic, mechanical, magnetic, and photographic,
including photocopying, recording or by any information storage and
retrieval system, without prior written permission of the publisher.

No patent liability is assumed with respect to the use of the information
contained herein. Although every precaution has been taken in the prepa-
ration of this book, the publisher and author assume no responsibility
for errors or omissions. Neither is any liability assumed for damages
resulting from the use of the information contained herein.

Unless otherwise noted, Scripture quotations are taken from the Holy Bible, New
International Version®, NIV®. Copyright © 1973, 1978, 1984, 2011 by Biblica,
Inc.® Used by permission of Zondervan. All rights reserved worldwide. www.
zondervan.com. The "NIV" and "New International Version" are trademarks
registered in the United States Patent and Trademark Office by Biblica, Inc.®

Scripture quotations marked NASB1995 are taken from the New American Standard
Bible® (NASB). Copyright © 1960, 1962, 1963, 1968, 1971, 1972, 1973, 1975, 1977,
1995 by The Lockman Foundation. Used by permission. www.Lockman.org.

Scripture quotations marked NKJV are taken from the New King James Version®.
Copyright © 1982 by Thomas Nelson. Used by permission. All rights reserved.

Published by Forefront Books.

Cover Design by EPIC
Interior Design by Bill Kersey, KerseyGraphics

ISBN: 978-1-63763-069-3 print
ISBN: 978-1-63763-070-9 e-book

*To the courageous men who have gone ALL IN
to look into their own lives at our retreats and forums
and found healing, freedom, and their deeper calling.*

*One hundred percent of the proceeds from the sale of this
book go to the charitable foundation supporting
ALL IN to help men in their journey to freedom.*

contents

acknowledgments

To my insightful best friend, partner, and wife, June, who encouraged me to finally "write this book to help more men . . . and women." How many good things happen because of the encouragement of one person!

To my beloved children, Olivia, Lisel, Mallori, and Spencer, who impress me every day, who share my love for the adventure of learning and life, and who continue to be my teachers.

A special thanks to my editor, David Kopp, who made me a better writer and who has lived and understands this journey himself. And to my tireless, excellent assistant, Karen Fitzgerald, for enduring my endless editing.

foreword

*L*EADERSHIP IS BOTH A PRIVILEGE AND A RESPONSI-
bility. To inspire others to perform at high levels
requires the very best abilities of the individual to imagine,
strategize, and connect.

It can be an exciting and fulfilling ride. At the same time,
as one who works almost exclusively with leaders, I have
found that most leaders at some point hit certain walls. It's
almost inevitable. It can be the wall of not performing at
one's best. Or the wall of struggling relationships. Or the
wall of troubling feelings, thoughts, and habits.

Unfortunately, most leaders do not have the information they need to know what to do next. In my experience,
most resort to the "put-head-down-and-move-forward"
strategy, which is a form of willpower. They work harder
and try to work smarter. They try to stay positive and keep
their chins up.

All these tactics for getting back in the game do have
value, but they are actually minor elements in what leaders
actually need.

Allen Morris's book *All In* provides very significant
and helpful answers that will make a profound difference.

He shows a key obstacle to a leader's personal and professional success is *the unknown and unacknowledged presence of thoughts, memories, and emotions that hamper and often sabotage us*. Put another way, that which we have not been able to face and deal with from our past has enormous power over our future.

Allen draws deeply from his own experience to make his case. At the peak of a highly successful career in real estate, Allen began experiencing debilitating struggles that limited him in many ways, both professionally and personally. Though he tried to "put head down and move forward," nothing worked.

It was not until he was able to deal with his own past and his own unknown that he could free himself for a new season of high performance, great relationships, and emotional happiness. I won't spoil this for you, but Allen's story alone makes this book more than worth the read.

All In draws from many sources, including research, (his own and other leaders' experiences), psychology, and the Bible. On that score, psychiatrist Carl Jung's concept of the shadow is a foundational aspect of Allen's approach. The shadow is described by Jung as the part of our subconscious mind where we hide taboo or unwanted thoughts, feelings, and desires. Contrary to some stereotypes, it does not equal the "bad" aspects of us but simply the "unknown" aspects. We have stored them, usually because of overwhelming hurt, loss, or trauma. They are then simply ignored because we do not have the strength or skills to understand, process, and release them.

Leaders can find these concepts confusing. But current neuroscience and trauma research validate that unknown aspects of our minds, when not attended to, play a significant role in our lives. This understanding is corroborated by biblical teachings—for example, that God "knows the secrets of the heart" (Psalm 44:21 NKJV).

In fact, there is a wealth of neuroscience research specifically targeted to leadership that validates many of this book's conclusions.

In addition to exploring these important concepts, the book provides a practical, tested, and hope-filled approach for applying them. ALL IN, the organization that Allen founded, sponsors meetings and retreats where leaders can experience safe, supportive, and nonjudgmental opportunities to identify and deal successfully with the experiences and distortions coming from their shadows. Allen's book tells the stories of men who have literally found new, transformative beginnings through doing the work.

This is where the title *All In* is key. Leaders do well to commit themselves wholly to their own growth—and that means being "all in." Yes, it takes time, effort, and vulnerability, but the rewards are truly worth it. We are, as the book's subtitle states, risking everything for everything that matters because what matters most to us is a life of purpose, great relationships, meaningful achievement, and emotional health. Compared to these benefits, the price is small.

One of the key insights of the book is the necessity of supportive and vulnerable relationships. Most leaders I know have far too few of these, often limited to God, a loving spouse, a Labrador retriever, and some golf buddies. But we need more. We need a few good peers with whom we are willing to be real and travel alongside on the path to growth and change.

And the path that Allen lays out works.

On a personal note: Allen Morris has been a trusted and close friend of mine for many years. He has shared his narrative and his path with me, and I know him as a man who lives in integrity. His life is an example of how being "all in" to the process of transformation means you can win in all the areas of life that truly matter.

John Townsend, Ph.D.
New York Times *bestselling author*
of the Boundaries *book series*
Founder, Townsend Institute for Leadership and
Counseling, and Townsend Leadership Program
Laguna Beach, California
2022

CHAPTER 1

the view from the top

There was a man all alone.

—KING SOLOMON

THEY SAY A MAN IS KNOWN BY THE COMPANY HE keeps. I tend to keep company with men who know how to make things happen. These men bring the incredible skills and immense drive it takes to compete and to win. Like Thoroughbreds on race day quivering in their starting stalls, they know that *running to win* is what they're made to do.

And run, they do.

A champion competitor performing in his element is a beautiful thing to watch. Off like thunder at the starting gate, straining with every muscle to dominate in the turns, powering through the back stretch, and crossing the finish line ... *first*.

Because who wants to come in second place?

The makers, leaders, and entrepreneurs who take risks for a living have been my peers and close friends throughout my forty years as a CEO. I know what gets these finely tuned strivers and achievers up in the morning, and I know what keeps them going late at night.

Whatever they do, professionally at least, they're *all in*.

These super achievers are some of the most gifted and well-intentioned people you could hope to meet, and they're surrounded by impressive proofs of success: multiple mansions ... stylish yachts ... sleek personal jets.

But I've also come to know that, inside, many of these same people feel something less than successful and free. Often a lot less. Hard to believe, isn't it? In fact, many do not feel like winners at all. Instead, many successful men feel empty and trapped in a world of their own creation.

I know this because when these men feel safe—*when they trust that I get it and that I care* (and will definitely keep my mouth shut!)—they have let me into their hidden struggles.

What they often feel most profoundly is alone.[1]

Or stuck and craving freedom.[2]

Which raises a very important question: How do men who aspire to excellence, and who outwardly may appear to have it in spades, come to terms with the forces that hold them back from true happiness and fulfillment and then decide to do the hard work required for real change and freedom? How do they begin to grow into the thriving, wholehearted men they sincerely want to be?

> When I was forty-seven years old and at the top of my world, I made the surprising discovery that my little kingdom was already crumbling.

That's what this book is about.

When I was forty-seven years old and at the top of my world—or so I thought—I made the surprising discovery that my little kingdom was already crumbling, the first cracks in the mortar starting with me. What had worked for me for years as a CEO, husband, and father stopped working. It seemed so sudden, but as I gradually realized, I just hadn't been paying attention. That guy who felt alone, stuck, afraid, and ashamed? That was me.

I was hurting. Worse, people closest to me—the ones I loved the most—were hurting.

Hurting bad.

And I take the blame for most of it.

But at the time I wondered what had happened to my dream life. I had no clue. Who was this person, Allen Morris—*really*—beyond what you could read in his "impressive" real estate development bio? Suddenly I didn't know much about that anymore either.

If you've ever found yourself at this kind of crossroad, you know what it's like to make some of the toughest choices of your life.

Looking back now, I see that season of crisis as an enormous gift. It set me in motion on an inward journey—call it a journey into the hidden self—that required going where I didn't want to go and seeing what I didn't want to see. Some insights from that experience shocked and saddened me yet ultimately opened the door to new freedom and joy.

Insights such as this: *You can go amazingly far in life, winning trophies left and right, without ever reckoning with the actual cost of your success and who is paying the price.*

And this: *The very same skills, values, and mindset that catapult you up in life can also bring you crashing down.*

the lonely whine of the top dog

When I look back on the person I used to be, I couldn't be more grateful. Sometimes the end of something is the best kind of beginning. At least you get to start working on what matters most before it's too late.

King Solomon, as you may remember, rose to the very pinnacle of the ancient world with wealth, fame, wisdom, and power. And let's not forget his palace full of wives and mistresses.

By any measure, he had it made.

But Solomon discovered that the view from the top let him see into the heart of things, and what he saw troubled him deeply. He concluded that men are driven to succeed largely out of envy and rivalry, which he thought explained why so many high achievers end up lonely and discontented.

"There was a man all alone," he wrote, obviously writing about himself. "There was no end to his toil, yet his eyes were not content with his wealth." What it all added up to, he decided, was "meaningless—a miserable business!"[3]

> He scaled the ladder of accomplishments… only to discover his ladder was leaning against the wrong wall.

You could say he scaled the ladder of accomplishments all the way to the top rung, only to discover his ladder was leaning against the wrong wall. A writer I admire called this kind of emptiness in the midst of apparent success "the lonely whine of the top dog."

Because of my work over forty years with hundreds of focused, hard-charging leaders, I can relate. Maybe you can too. No matter how we may appear in the boardroom or when relaxing with friends, many of us feel caught in a tangle of paradoxes.

We crave freedom yet we wish we felt more connected in our relationships.

We prize authenticity yet too often we feel like imposters just hoping we don't get found out.

We think we're as smart as, or smarter than, the next guy yet we seem to struggle more than most to understand our wife or partner and our children.

We genuinely want to be good men yet some days we feel defined by powerful desires that threaten to harm us and those we love.

If you see yourself in these struggles, I understand if you feel doomed to flounder in the dark.

But that is not the case.

journey into the unknown

This is a book for men who are ready to explore the terra incognita of their hidden self in order to achieve the life they deeply want.

In the pages ahead, I invite you into my story and the stories of other leaders I've met on this journey. Because in our experience, no simplistic solution is as helpful as another well-traveled man's honestly shared truth.

Our guideposts on this journey are age-old questions every man understands:

+ *Why do I so often feel dissatisfied and unfulfilled?*
+ *Why do certain confounding, logic-defying behaviors repeatedly leave me feeling stuck?*
+ *Can I ever experience the freedom I crave?*

And one more:

+ *What am I willing to risk to be free?*

We have discovered that whenever a man sets out to achieve transformation at this level, the trajectory of his life will follow a pattern. Not a formula, mind you, or a new belief system, but a journey into unexplored territory that is recognized across cultures. It's been called the Hero's Journey because the traveler must be willing to leave the known, travel toward what he does not know, and engage in a high-stakes battle with his own darkness before he can return home a changed man.

For every man I know, the last and greatest blank space in our lives is our own undiscovered self. The Swiss psychiatrist Carl G. Jung first used the term *shadow self* to describe the part of our subconscious where we hide taboo or unwanted thoughts, memories, feelings, and desires. As we'll see, it's also where we stuff all the fears, pain, and wounds from our past: unresolved and broken relationships, judgments, self-hatred, disappointments, injuries, abuse, and addictions.[4]

> "Until you make the unconscious conscious, it will direct your life and you will call it fate." -Carl Jung

Since in practical terms the word *subconscious* means "outside of our awareness," we can easily go through life entirely unaware of the existence of the shadow self, or simply "the shadow," and what's hidden there. Which means, of course, that we're oblivious to how this unconscious part of ourselves is driving our conscious decisions.[5]

This is where "confounding" and "logic defying" come in.

As Jung wrote, "Until you make the unconscious conscious, it will direct your life and you will call it fate."[6]

Especially for men in their middle years who have been carrying a lifelong burden of unresolved pain, fear, guilt, or resentment, the burden can trickle out in lapses, indiscretions, and tenacious and unwanted habits.

Or it can explode out of the dark with devastating consequences.

"It is often tragic to see how blatantly a man bungles his own life and the lives of others," Jung wrote, "yet remains totally incapable of seeing how much the whole tragedy originates in himself, and how he continually feeds it and keeps it going."[7]

This book is not meant to be a technical exploration of the role of the subconscious in our lives, although there is strong neuroscience data to support it.[8] Rather, my purpose and passion here is to deliver a "whole life" exploration for leaders who need transformation.

To help us on our way, I draw on a wide range of sources —psychologists, psychiatrists, spiritual writers, Jung's insights, the Bible, and most especially, our shared stories. I introduce you to our work at ALL IN and show you what happens when men search for answers in the company of like-minded men who can help us find and speak our truth.

It's a journey with risks and pitfalls, for sure. Yet it holds incredible promise for growth and change both in our professional and personal lives.

In my forty years as a member of the Young Presidents Organization (YPO) and its graduate organization, YPO Gold, I have come to know hundreds of CEOs, many of them very well. It seems to be a consistent theme that long-term business success and personal fulfillment are ultimately a reflection of, and dependent on, a leader's emotional health.

No wonder Solomon advised, "Above all else, guard your heart, for everything you do flows from it."[9]

facing death and life in winter park

One of my mentors, a great and inspiring man whom I considered like an uncle, was a history-making entrepreneur and CEO. He founded a worldwide nonprofit organization with a staff of twenty thousand and one hundred thousand volunteers in 190 countries. He wrote more than thirty books, and I admired him for his spiritual depth and theological insights. As a young man, I had the pleasure of working as his assistant during a conference in South Korea that drew an audience—I kid you not—of a million people. Many years later, I chaired his national program for executive leaders.

His name was Bill Bright.

One day in the fall of 2000, about nine months after I'd begun my personal journey, Dr. Bright called to tell me he had been diagnosed with a terminal illness. The news was heartbreaking. When he asked if I would come and visit him, I jumped at the invitation.

As Bill and I walked along the shaded sidewalks of Park Avenue in Winter Park, he told me more about his illness. It was pulmonary fibrosis. Before too long, it would steal his ability to breathe. Despite the seriousness of his condition, Bill told me he was delaying a trip to Denver for treatment. "You know, I'm finding it hard to fit treatment into my schedule," he said.

I couldn't believe my ears! Then again, I could. Here was a man who had committed his entire life to bringing spiritual renewal to the world, and even now at death's doorstep, he couldn't imagine slowing down.

After walking and talking for a while, we found a bench and Bill asked me to bring him up to date on my story. What new ventures was I pursuing these days?

I thought, *Well, here goes!* He might not like it, but I wanted to tell him my whole truth.

"Allen, you must write a book about this! You could help so many men!"

I shared with Bill—as I will with you in the pages ahead—how my personal and work lives had become so painful. The failing relationships. The impossible expectations. The weird awareness that I didn't know what I was feeling, except that I felt lousy.

Even though I knew he was skeptical of psychology and self-help, I diagrammed for him the circle of light and dark—a picture of the interior life I was finding incredibly helpful.

I told him how I wanted to know what made so many talented, focused, decent men self-destruct in a big way. Because, yeah, I feared I might be one of those too.

Still, I told him, I was beginning to believe again that freedom, healing, and passion might—just *might*—be possible for a man in my circumstance. That I could rekindle a deep sense of power and joy.

Then I "fessed up" to the unthinkable: I had virtually walked out on my own career until I could find answers.

I braced myself for Bill's response.

Instead of caution and criticism, he lit up with excitement. He leaned toward me and said, "Allen, you must write a book about this! You could help so many men!"

I said, "But Bill, I couldn't even scratch out a preface for a book! I'm still figuring it out for myself."

I've spent the twenty-plus years since that conversation "figuring it out" enough to write this book and share what I've learned firsthand.

If you want a clinical manual or expert psychologist, well, that's not me. What I am is a fellow traveler and truth-teller with a particular passion for leaders in business, ministry, and the professions. Many of us have come to suspect that our drive for achievement and accomplishment may be out of control, bringing us and those we love more harm than we ever thought possible.

Your story and mine will differ, of course. Our beliefs, resources, and front-burner issues will vary, too, but the very fact that you're reading this page convinces me we are meant to connect—that we already speak the same language.

Wherever you are on your journey, whatever you're trying to move through, away from, or closer to, I'm confident you'll find resources in these pages that will become game changers for you. An authentic telling of our stories is how cultures have always passed along their most enduring gifts.

You are about to experience what happens when you take your place in a circle of like-minded men, each broken in different places, who take risks to share their deepest truths, listen well, and stand alongside one another in solidarity, believing heart and soul in one another's worth.

Welcome to your journey. There is good news ahead.

pause to reflect

1. What part of this chapter seems to stick with you the most? Consider what that might tell you about a potential growth area for you.

2. What would an "all in, hold nothing back" version of you look like at home? At work?

3. So many words and ideas in this chapter are packed with promise: "rekindle," "shared stories," "healing," "Hero's Journey," "freedom," "crossroad," "real change," "thriving." Pick one and consider holding it in your thoughts or meditation this week.

For more free resources, see

CHAPTER 2

something
isn't working

The mass of men lead lives of quiet desperation.

—Henry David Thoreau

The relentless, piercing headaches began suddenly and continued day and night for two weeks. Just to get by, I'd take two extra-strength Excedrin at 10:00 p.m., wake up with a splitting headache at 2:00 a.m., take two more Excedrin, then wake up at 6:00 with another splitting headache, and then take two more Excedrin to start my day. I wasn't doing much more than crawling through my days pill by pill.

Something wasn't right.

I couldn't for the life of me understand where these headaches were coming from or why they had arrived at such an inconvenient time.

Excuse me, did he say brain tumor? My brain tumor?

My precious teenage daughter was going through a rebellious stage. It was February, and I had just come back from dropping her off at a boarding school in the frozen north of Vermont. On the two-hour drive back to the Burlington airport, I wept alone in the car, feeling like the worst father in the world.

Why my daughter was so angry, I couldn't say. I aspired to be a great dad. I read parenting books. I loved her and my other three kids. I prayed for them continually.

All right, I worked late most evenings building my business, but when I wasn't working or traveling, or stressing about working or traveling, I thought I gave my kids plenty of time and attention.

Why couldn't I fix this?

I *hated* feeling like a failure!

Two weeks of headaches was enough to get me to my doctor. Fortunately, he happened to be the head of the neurosurgery department at the hospital.

Sitting across from me in the examining room, he listened patiently to the details of my pain, asked some probing questions, then set me up for an MRI and a CAT scan at the first opening. Clearly, he was concerned, but at least he had a plan.

As I was about to leave, he said, "Allen, the imaging tests will show us what's going on. But I should warn you. Based on your symptoms, I believe we're looking at a brain tumor. If that's the case, the MRI will show us where your tumor is and from that we'll figure out treatment options."

Excuse me, did he say brain tumor? My brain tumor?

The MRI led to a CAT scan. Between the appointments and waiting for results, I had nearly three weeks to contemplate.

And contemplate some more.

picture perfect ... almost

On the outside, my personal life looked downright enviable. I owned and led a prestigious business developing, managing, and owning office buildings all over Florida. At that time, our company's seventy-ninth construction project was going up in the absolute finest location in Miami. To support our growth, my company also owned a successful real estate brokerage and property management business.

I was educated at Georgia Tech and Harvard Business School. I had strong spiritual values, and I'd been an elder in my church for twenty years. I even wrote a book on evidence for faith. Despite my already busy life, I found time to fly my own airplane, travel the world, and work into my schedule some public speaking engagements that I really enjoyed.

My wife was in charge of our home life, and I assumed all was well and that she was tending to the needs of our children. Four kids running around the house is a lot to handle, and I was proud to be able to support the household financially so that she could be home with them full-time.

But the tumor changed everything. It opened me up to the idea that the end of my life might be fast approaching. It's as though the blinders were taken off my eyes, allowing me to see things in a new way. With clear eyes, I moved closer to the truth of my life than I ever had before. Beyond the glossy appearances. Beyond the fancy bio, the glowing media coverage in the business pages, and my Sunday morning version of how things were going.

What I saw was *not* so great.

For years, we had enjoyed a very happy marriage, but things began to change. My wife, for example, always seemed stressed out. She wanted to be the perfect wife and mother, but she had her own pain. Some days, she locked herself in her room to cry. I could never figure out why, and she wouldn't say. She sometimes forgot to pick the kids up from school and even left them alone in the house. When I was away on business, I had no idea what was going on.

We had gone to at least six marriage seminars together. I had read books on marriage. With my bachelor's degree in psychology, I felt that I should have been smart enough to understand what was going on with her and fix our relationship. Instead, things at home left me feeling really stupid. (I learned years later that my wife was in the beginning stages of early-onset Alzheimer's disease, which could explain some if not most of what was going on.)

My children were feeling the stress in their own ways—struggling academically or with authority, or simply showing the hurt of feeling alone.

Meanwhile, at work there was a long-running conflict on my leadership team between two of my senior executives who were locked in a silent war that caused bottlenecks, duplication of efforts, and—beneath the surface of a pleasant office veneer—a generally miserable working environment. So far, I had mostly led by looking the other way, hoping for the best. One of the men drank too much, but, I reasoned, he was smart and it didn't seem to affect his work.

> So far, I had mostly led by looking the other way, hoping for the best.

Sure, I was the CEO and owner, so I could have done something about it, but I had let the situation go on for so long that I felt trapped—and secretly ashamed.

One more thing: both executives knew that I didn't think I could run the business without them.

CEO or not, I was walking on eggshells.

When I slowed down enough to take a good, hard look, I could see that my company was broken, starting at the top.

alien invader

Three weeks later, my doctor walked into the same examining room looking perplexed and—what was it—dejected? Like a child whose balloon deflated.

"Allen, I've consulted the radiologist and examined the films myself, and your tumor is ... not there!"

I immediately thought, *If it's not there, why are you calling it "my tumor"?*

Then he offered plan B. "I can prescribe muscle relaxants, beta-blockers, and pain meds. That should get the headaches under control."

Which wasn't really what I wanted to hear. "You're telling me that you can see no physical cause for my headaches," I said, "but you're giving me prescriptions to mask my pain?"

> If there is no physical cause for my pain, then I must be creating it myself somehow.

"Well, yes, that's about it," he said. "I don't doubt that the pain is real. But the test results are clear. Your brain is fine. I don't know what else to tell you."

I drove back to my office in a wrestling match with a brand-new thought that I didn't like one bit. *If there is no physical cause for my pain, then I must be creating it myself somehow.*

I really struggled to wrap my mind around that one. *How could I be creating it myself?*

Frankly, a part of me was disappointed that the tumor had vanished and left me with no physical enemy to take on, no hero's opportunity to defeat the alien invader in my body.

When I stood in front of a mirror and tried out a version of a "my real problem is me" speech, the CEO in me practically choked.

I didn't know where to begin, or how, or where I could turn for help. What I did know was that I was in pain.

Blinding *physical* pain from the mysterious headaches and the deep *emotional* ache of feeling disconnected from and in conflict with my family.

Pain, too, from feeling trapped in the stubbornly unresolvable conflict on my leadership team.

> When I tried out a version of a "my real problem is me" speech, the CEO in me practically choked.

Soon the kernel of a plan began to take shape.

I would take the meds the neurosurgeon had scripted—some of them anyway. But I had to uncover what was really wrong. It felt like a life-or-death matter. I needed to make this investigation my full-time journey and my number one job.

I had to go *all in*.

Ironically, I had recently concluded my term as chairman of the state chapter for the YPO. During my time at the helm, we had brought in resource people for CEOs who needed "that kind of help."

That kind of help for those kinds of fellows, I'd thought to myself at the time.

Well, clearly, I was now one of them.

You've noticed that I like to think that I am an intelligent, educated, perceptive person. I pride myself on knowing things and making things happen. That's how businesses like mine flourish. But I'll be honest, it wasn't the smart, insightful, performing side of me that determined what would happen next.

It was the pain.

what do you call a quitter?

Pain drove me to consider an unthinkable possibility: I might need to let go of my prestigious position as the "boss in control" of my own company.

And to find the time and energy to sort out my problem, the move could not be in name only. I would have to step away from all my leadership responsibilities at the company as well as step down from my positions on community boards and at church.

Right there in our kitchen, a solution popped out like a cork from a bottle of champagne—*sabbatical!*

This sounds funny to me now, but the final sticking point at the time was the question of what to tell people. I agonized over that. How could I explain a disappearing act to my colleagues? To my bankers and key business partners? To the community? How could I explain it to myself? I went round and round.

Was I afraid of looking irresponsible? Or like a quitter or childish? Would people think I was weak or mentally unfit? Did I worry people would think I had a terminal disease or a humiliating secret problem?

The answer was yes. All of the above. I hadn't been entirely aware until then how important my image and reputation were to me.

Thankfully, as I discussed things with my wife at that time, she seemed to understand. She said she wanted the same thing—to escape from the bone-crushing, oppressive, overcommitted life we had created for ourselves. So we agreed on the need, but neither of us knew what to call my next move.

Then, right there in our kitchen, a solution popped out like a cork from a bottle of champagne—*sabbatical!*

That was it! Wimps quit. But thoughtful, well-adjusted people took sabbaticals.

It was something I could tell people, and a word my secretary could use to explain my absence in the constant flow of communications with callers, clients, vendors, employees, community fundraisers, and charities.

A sabbatical would be my hiding place, a cave of safety I could retreat to while I figured out my life.

In short order I called a former senior VP of our company who had been working as a consultant to come in and take over as the managing director of the Allen Morris Company. I had decided to take a sabbatical, I told him. Effective immediately. I needed to step away from my business for a spell in order to save my life.

I figured if I had a real brain tumor, I would've been out of the picture pretty fast. This way, if somebody else ran the company into the ground, I would still be alive and could step back in to save it. Because, of course, I knew I was indispensable.

Yeah, sure.

Simultaneously, I hired a CEO coach/counselor for myself. He came highly recommended, required a one-year, no-cut contract paid in advance. If I fired him, the unused portion of his annual contract would go to a charity of my choice. With one exclusion. He stipulated it could not go to my own charity, The Allen Morris Foundation.

I thought I was a tough negotiator, but this guy was impossible! I guess he knew I was a hard-core case. Or maybe he didn't want me to waste his time if I wasn't absolutely serious.

On Friday, March 13, I sat at my desk in the penthouse of the 1000 Brickell Building in Miami with my new managing director and agreed to his terms.

The following Monday, I made the announcement to my executive team.

Tuesday, I traded in my office and the responsibilities that went with it for my new "job"—journaling over coffee at an out-of-the-way diner called the Ugly Tuna Saloon.

I was desperate. Physically and emotionally, I simply wasn't up to what life was requiring of me, and I didn't know why. Mostly, what I did not know was ... *myself*.

The journey was about to begin. My original deal with the former senior VP—now my managing director—was intended to last for three months. I could never have imagined it at the time, but those three months would turn into three amazing years.

pause to reflect

1. All of us feel pain every day in some way—body, emotions, memories. But often our busy lives don't allow us to pay attention. Where do you most tend to *overlook* or *ignore* pain in your day-to-day life?

2. How well do you feel your life is working right now? If you have some concerns, what are they? And how might your wife, your children, or your closest friend answer those questions for you?

3. Do you feel the need for a meaningful sabbatical experience? What would you want that to look like, and how would you want it to affect you? What's stopping you from making it happen?

For more free resources, see

CHAPTER 3

waking up to what's inside

There is no coming to consciousness without pain.

—CARL JUNG

O N THE FIRST DAY OF MY "NEW LIFE," I FELT LIBER-
ated. Instead of my standard white shirt, cuff links,
dark suit, and tie, I now had "permission" to dress in cargo
pants and a button-down shirt. I also grew a beard and
developed an overall relaxed exterior. That part was fun.

Right away, I started meeting with my coach. He
proposed four-hour meetings during which I would identify my issues and he would give me assignments. On my
own time, he wanted me to start filling journals with my
thoughts.

He asked what we were
feeling; I kept answering
with what I was *thinking*.

I found a close-by neighborhood
diner I had never set foot inside
before, where no one I knew would
go. I spent hours there in "my booth"
ordering coffee and iced tea, and
writing, writing, writing—watching
the words and thoughts flow from
my mind to the page. Thoughts about
my childhood, my parents, my sisters, my children, my wife,
and my life up to that point. Thoughts I didn't know were
there until they came out on paper.

My coach was kind enough not to put a label on what
I was doing. If he had, it might have been "Homework in
Self-Awareness."

But more probably, "Baby Steps for Clueless Middle-
Aged Dude Who Finally Wants to Get a Clue."

Fortunately, my work with him paralleled much of
what my YPO group was offering at the time. In an
early retreat, we sat in the circle with our facilitator, who

asked us a bewildering question: "What are you feeling right now?"

That was not a question I or (as far as I could tell) the other seven men in the circle had grown up with. Internally, I responded like the proverbial deer in headlights.

What do you mean, "What am I feeling?!"

I could tell him what I thought and what I believed. I could identify my convictions and values. I could say what needed to be done and by whom and when.

But what I feel? That, I didn't know.

He asked again, "What are you feeling?"

"I feel fine," someone volunteered.

"If fine were a feeling, what would that look like?" he asked.

"Like I said, fine."

The conversation in my head ramped up: *I feel like this discussion is a waste of time. I'd like to know what our agenda is. I'd like to know what our objectives are for this time together ... Doesn't he know this feelings stuff is for women and children?*

But the facilitator would not let us off the hook until we understood the distinction I was resisting: he had asked what we were *feeling*; I kept answering with what I was *thinking*.

Then he took us further. He pointed out inconsistencies between what we said we wanted and what we actually did. In other words, general feelings versus specific actions. See if you can relate:

• I wanted to lose weight, but I kept eating desserts.

- I wanted to get in shape, but I rarely worked out.
- I wanted quality time with my family, but I could not get out of the office in time to get home for dinner.
- I wanted more freedom and margin in my work, but I continued to obsessively control details and take on more responsibilities and volunteer for more community service assignments.

It became irritatingly apparent that I was not the person I thought I was. I was not clear, focused, or in control.

Back working with my personal coach, I followed the trail of disconnections and inconsistencies even further.

I discovered that while I might want to lose weight, there was a powerful reason I would order the dessert. I needed help with *a feeling I did not want to feel*. In this case, I was feeling stressed or lonely or worried, and I wanted to soothe and reward myself with, say, a slice of Key lime pie or an extra glass of wine, because, you know, I deserved it. I discovered my stomach was my teacher, and it has continual messages for me if I will listen.

It became irritatingly apparent that I was not the person I thought I was.

But what was the feeling underneath that thought?

I discovered *stronger feelings* guiding, or misdirecting, my path. For example, I might want to get home from the office to have dinner with my family, but I would keep working because I wanted even more to feel the self-worth of accomplishment of completing a task—whether urgent or not. Or I would feel such resentment that I had let someone take me off-task earlier in the day that I felt I deserved to have the right to finish my task now.

I discovered *influential but unnamed feelings*. I might think and say something was important to me, but I wouldn't do it because, under the surface and unbeknownst to me, I was feeling something quite different. For example, anxiety about how acting on that feeling would be received.

Whether in large or small matters, I began to see that feelings drove me more than I ever knew. In my work. In my relationships. In my community service. In my family. Which led me to a somewhat shocking, and possibly universal, truth: *I may say and think and believe one thing, but in the end, I'm going to do what I feel.*

> **I may say and think and believe one thing, but in the end, I'm going to do what I feel.**

For me, it was a conclusion that required action. If I never learned to be aware of my own emotional universe, then a part of me would go on undiscovered yet would ultimately determine my fate. Wouldn't that be dumb, maybe even dangerous?

the world underneath

At the beginning of my quest, I was such a hopeless case that my coach gave me a 3 × 5 card to carry in my pocket. It listed six feelings:

Mad, Glad, Sad, Tender, Excited, Scared

"I want you to look at this card five hundred times a day and ask yourself, 'What am I feeling right now?'" he instructed.

Okay, so I did it only ten times a day, but it was like torture for me. It was like exercising those little muscles in your shoulder you rarely use but must warm up before you start your upper-body lifting routine.

When I realized how separated I lived from my feelings, I saw that I had become more of a human *doing* than a human *being*.

> I had become more of a human *doing* than a human *being*.

Of course, feelings are not everything, and they're as changeable as the weather—but they're not nothing either! Like a thermometer, a feeling can point to something you might not see: a sickness, say, or a lingering infection. Like the check-engine light on your car, feelings can make you aware of a potential threat.

I just kept pulling out that 3 × 5 card—during my morning reflection, after a phone call from the office, after a conversation with one of my children—and I kept asking the question, *What am I feeling right now?*

More often than not, what I was feeling was anxious, worried, concerned, irritated, or frustrated. Not too hard. But that was just a beginning.

Those everyday feelings led me to deeper insight: all of those feelings seemed to fall into two categories—angry or scared.

I didn't like those words—especially the thought that they might apply to me. Because how could they? I was courageous to a fault. I would go scuba diving to hundred-foot-plus depths to explore rusty old shipwrecks. I piloted a jet at forty-five thousand feet. I drove race cars and rode motorcycles.

As a black belt, I broke four boards at a time with my fists.

Daily, it was my job to roll the dice on major multimillion-dollar real estate developments.

But that was my exterior talking. I discovered that simmering underneath it all was fear. Allen the CEO, father, and husband was scared—a lot. Not the whimpering-in-public kind of scared but nonetheless a man driven too often by fear.

All of those feelings seemed to fall into two categories—angry or scared.

Maybe all those adrenaline-pumping activities were an effort to prove to myself that I was a manly man. Courageous, accomplished, and worthy.

your daughter is your teacher

Early in my process of awakening to feelings, I told my coach about a conversation I had with one of my daughters when she was eleven years old. At the time, I struggled to feel close to her, and it didn't help that she seemed gloomy a lot.

Things came to a head one December evening while my wife and I were hosting our annual Christmas party for 150 community leaders and old friends. I got an urgent message that my daughter, who I thought was asleep upstairs, had become ill. A friend of my daughter and her mother, who was a nurse, went upstairs to be with her and provide help. Nobody at the party knew what was going on upstairs and thought the night was a big success.

As the last of our company drove away, I finally ran upstairs to check on my daughter.

Right away I saw that she was much sicker than I had realized. And much more upset with me too.

"Dad!" she wailed, tearful and angry. "You don't care about me, do you? You don't understand what I'm going through!"

But I was ready. Drawing on my undergraduate degrees in psychology and training in counseling, I replied, "Sweetie, nobody can really understand what another person is feeling."

At the time, I thought it was a stunning insight. I also thought it a mark of good leadership that I had delegated my daughter's emergency care to someone else so that my annual Christmas party could continue uninterrupted. After all, the show must go on.

It took years of working with my coach before I could look back on that evening and sort out what was really going on. But at the time, I didn't understand my own feelings, which meant I certainly couldn't empathize with my daughter's, much less realize how off the mark I was as a dad.

The incident showcased not my executive skills but my incompetence. More precisely, my *emotional incompetence*.

No wonder I had "delegated" sending my daughter away to boarding school so that my life could also continue "uninterrupted" by the conflict and chaos I could not understand or control.

After I told my tale of woe to my coach, I expected some affirmation for making progress. But he simply responded, "Your daughter is your teacher. She is your mirror to help you see the truth about yourself."

At first, I was shocked. What could he possibly mean? *I'm* the parent here!

But as days and weeks went by, his words stayed with me. Today, I can assure you that my coach's shocking statement has been a gift that I have continued to unwrap in the years since.

> "Everything that irritates us about others can lead us to an understanding of ourselves." *-Jung*

As Jung observed, "Everything that irritates us about others can lead us to an understanding of ourselves."[10] My daughter and I laugh about it now, and I continue to refer to her as "my teacher" because she still is in many important and uplifting ways.

There's an old-time fable of the farmer who sold his mule and plow to a neighbor. The farmer promised that, unlike most mules, this one was very obedient.

But in no time at all, the neighbor brought the mule back, and he was furious. "Obedient?" he yelled. "Who are you kiddin'? I can't get that stubborn beast to do *a single damn thing* he don't want to!"

"Uh-huh," said the farmer calmly. "Let me show you something." He picked up a two-by-four and whacked the mule along the side of the head, after which the mule began obediently pulling the plow.

"See what I'm sayin'?" he told his neighbor. "That mule's very obedient. You just have to get his attention first!"

I don't recommend abusing livestock, but here's why I remember the mule story: God has used pain to get my attention. The anguish around my marriage and family helped open my eyes to see what I couldn't see before. The pain of my headaches made me stop what I was doing and notice that I was stuck and barely awake in my own life.

Sometimes we want to blame God for painful losses or unwanted circumstances, but I have found that they may in fact be a loving God's way of getting our attention. It has been for me.

As the Oxford scholar and professor C. S. Lewis wrote in *The Problem of Pain*, "God whispers to us in our pleasures, speaks in our conscience, but shouts in our pain: It is his megaphone to rouse a deaf world."[11]

paralyzed by fear

On one of our early YPO Forum retreats, our small group of men trekked into the desolate Mexican desert ranges of Baja California, where it seemed like fear tried to take us down at every turn. We were surrounded by a hostile environment, far from civilization, and with little chance of survival if we sustained a serious injury.

One morning I awoke in my bedroll (we slept on the ground) to find a six-foot rattlesnake coiled nearby, watching me with far too much interest, I thought.

Another guy discovered scorpions had taken up residence in his journal during the night.

After long days of adventure trekking, our facilitator would gather us around a campfire to debrief. He challenged us to consider the role of fear in keeping us from seeing painful but potentially liberating truths. The fears we were confronting in our outward surroundings, he said, could heighten our awareness of how fear could limit the inner journey we were being challenged to embrace.

My friend Al was *not* ready for such talk.

He was a very successful entrepreneur and CEO who had built and run a large medical equipment business. He was a leader in his church and champion of many good social ventures. But facing his fears in the company of other guys? No way.

At one point, he shouted across the campfire, "You guys may need this stuff, but this is not for me. This is bullshit!"

Without giving it much thought, I responded, "Al, your pain is just not great enough yet." Everyone erupted in laughter, and soon Al joined in the fun.

Pain as a heart excavator? Yes.

For Al, the experience in the desert was a turning point. He laughs as he tells that story on himself today. In the years since, he has helped many other men on their journey into self-awareness and healing.

You may be like me or Al, confident in your personal convictions, beliefs, and mission in life ... until the torpedo hits and rearranges everything.

In countless discussions with men in well over one hundred retreats, I have found that often ugly, unwanted pain—emotional, spiritual, or physical—is what drives us to see truths about ourselves we would otherwise miss. And the result can be transforming: a journey out of numbness and stuckness toward awareness, and beyond that to empathizing with and loving others genuinely and deeply.

will you do anything i ask?

After a couple of months of intensive work, my coach asked me an outrageous question, one no one had ever dared to ask me: "Will you do anything I ask you to?"

Sounded bizarre, actually! I couldn't imagine what freakish thing he might have in mind, but we had spent months building trust and by now I believed that he had my best interests at heart. Besides, if it was too crazy, I could just fire him.

I said, "Let me sleep on it before I decide." But the next day I said, "Okay. I'm willing to consider it. What is it?"

He said, "I want you to go to AA meetings—a lot of them. Sixty meetings in sixty days."

My immediate reaction was, "You can't be serious!"

"I'm deadly serious," he replied.

"But why Alcoholics Anonymous? I'm not an alcoholic!"

He said, "Because God is there."

But to me, those words felt like injury added to the insult. I needed to go to a meeting with the dregs of society *because* God is there? I needed more God?

What am I? I wanted to shout. *A godless reprobate?*

I had written a book on evidence for the faith.

I was an elder in my church, chairman of the board of a national Christian ministry, and the director of a very active local ministry to executives.

And this guy thought I needed to go to AA meetings?

Immediately I began to fret about what I was going to say if someone there recognized me. Which was likely to happen. After all, as CEO of a large company bearing my name in my community, I'm kind of a big fish in a little pond.

> Unwanted pain—emotional, spiritual, or physical—is what drives us to see truths about ourselves we would otherwise miss.

This could ruin my reputation.

The following week, at my YPO Forum retreat in Colorado, I shared my dilemma. Several of the men volunteered an immediate fix—they would *all* go with me to an AA meeting nearby. We were in Breckenridge, Colorado, and no one would recognize me.

My first meeting was spellbinding.

We listened to gut-wrenchingly honest stories from first one person, then another and another, whose lives had been destroyed by addiction. They had had everything, and then they lost it all to alcohol—businesses, homes, careers, marriages, families, friendships. And yet they just put their experiences of pain and loss out there, as though the stories themselves could be gifts to the rest of us, and maybe to them as well.

I realized I had never encountered a group like this. Men and women who brought no carefully manicured persona. No judgment. No advice. No fixing the other person. Just their own raw truth.

And it all happened in a circle of unconditional grace. Honestly, I'd never seen this in any church or Christian ministry, as loving and accepting as those places may have wished to be.

> They just put their experiences of pain and loss out there, as though the stories themselves could be gifts to the rest of us, and maybe to them as well.

The experience was mind-blowing. And I was intrigued.

I soon learned of the sister group, a 12-step recovery program called Al-Anon, which was a support group for friends and family of alcoholics. They humbly saw themselves as addicts too—just addicts of a different type. "Addicted enablers," they would say, who were also in need of recovery. At Al-Anon, as we listened to one another's stories, I discovered the same disarming honesty, attentiveness, and acceptance—all of it devoid of shaming or fixing.

I noticed that just being in that space was peacefully therapeutic for me.

Something similar happened when I journaled by myself at the diner. I seemed to need to write things down before I knew what I was feeling.

the circle of grace

Remember those headaches? Their frequency had lessened, but they still leveled me a couple of times a week. They would start with a tight feeling in the back of my head and always foretold a vicious attack of pain to come. Unless I took two Excedrin when I felt the warning signal, the head-aches would land with a vengeance every time.

It was around this time that my coach devised a new torture.

"Next time you feel the headache coming on, do not take your Excedrin. Just feel the headache and ask yourself, 'How am I creating this for myself?'"

I thought of lots of names to call him. And none of them was nice. I dreaded the pain I would have to endure. But by now I was more open to new ideas, no matter how torturous.

One Friday afternoon I had to go into the office for meetings and decisions I couldn't get out of, even though I was still on sabbatical. As the day wound down, I recog-nized the warning signal of an oncoming headache. The freight train that was about to hit.

I thought, *Okay, here it comes. I'm going to be a man and not take my meds.*

And I didn't. I pondered how I might be creating my headache, but I didn't have an answer.

By now, it was time for my Friday night Al-Anon meeting, so I went straight there. After sitting in that circle of grace for twenty minutes, I realized the alarm bell of pain I felt on the way to the meeting was ...gone. No headache.

That had *never* happened.

I was amazed and elated.

The breakthrough confirmed that I was on to something. I was, in fact, sitting in the middle of it—the healing power of acceptance in a loving, honest, compassionate, and empathetic community. No judgment, criticism, or how-to-fix-it advice. Just broken people like me sharing honestly about their struggles.

A true psychochemical reaction had occurred in my brain, and without the help of pharmaceuticals. That's when I became a believer in the healing powers of a circle of grace.

What else was there for me to see that I was not seeing?

pause to reflect

1. What are you feeling ... right now? Take several minutes to sit with that feeling, without judgment. Then write down what you're feeling in a few words.

2. Is there a feeling *underneath* that feeling? Take time to let it make itself known to you.

3. "Everything that irritates us about others," said Jung, "can lead us to an understanding of ourselves." Call to mind a recent strong irritation at work or home. Sit with it until you begin to see connections to *who you are*, *what you want*, or *what you fear*. What came to mind?

For more free resources, see

CHAPTER 4

troubling
revelations

*Codependence is driven by the agreement
that I will work harder on your problem and
your life than you do. This is not love.*

—DANNY SILK[12]

THE TRUTH IS, I FOUND THE WEEKLY 12-STEP MEET-ings a healing experience. They provided a time to slow down, listen, notice, and write down my feelings. Remember, this feeling stuff was still foreign to me and very hard to connect with.

After I finished sixty meetings in sixty days, I found myself going back anyway—two to three times a week, sometimes more—even though I sometimes I felt I was attending under false pretenses. I had no alcoholism in my world, at least that I was aware of.

One day after a meeting, I was walking out to my car when the realization hit me like I had walked into a plate glass window. Alcohol *was* undermining my life in the guise of the chief financial officer (CFO) of my company (whom I've already told you about). The problem wasn't his alcohol per se but who he was gradually becoming at work.

Which was a bottleneck for the whole organization.

He had become increasingly belligerent and obstruc-tive, and no one in the company could work with him. Of course, as the CFO he controlled all our money.

I had tried without luck to help him work more smoothly with others. Now that I was waking up to the unhealthy tendencies in my own life, I felt I was in a better place to encourage him to get help, maybe go into recovery. I did my best, but he refused. What could I do? I was afraid our whole accounting and finance and investments depart-ments would unravel if I fired him. He had convinced me that he was irreplaceable.

So I backed off. I felt ashamed and embarrassed about this, but I figured I was stuck. If I fired him, why wouldn't he use bank codes to transfer all our funds to Panama or Switzerland? I imagined all the worst possibilities.

We could be ruined. It was at this moment that I identified my feeling as "scared."

Addiction is an ugly word that gets thrown around too easily. There are many kinds of addictions: alcohol, drugs, gambling, sex, pornography, love, food, enabling, codependency, work, religion, perfectionism, and more.

Addictive behavior is anything that hurts us or those we love that we keep on doing anyway.

Most of us can see areas in our lives where we do something to excess from time to time, maybe regularly, and maybe in spite of negative consequences. And we don't know why. But the amazing human potential to get hooked on harmful substances and behaviors is something we all need to be aware of. I was certainly beginning to suspect that it played a larger role in my life and family than I had been willing to face.

The definition of addictive behavior I find most helpful is this: addictive behavior is anything that hurts us or those we love that we keep on doing anyway.

Please don't misunderstand what I mean by identifying addictive behavior around me in these wake-up moments. I don't mean to point fingers or sound harsh or judgmental. I was simply coming to awareness about hurting people I cared about and who depended on me. I was seeing addictiveness and its consequences in my own behavior.

And I was learning new, helpful language to talk about it.

the harm we do for goodness' sake

By now, my own part in the dysfunction at work was becoming clear. A couple of my behaviors—ones I frankly thought of as my superpowers—had recently revealed themselves as causing a world of hurt.

The first was my enormous need to rescue people and situations and to keep underperforming friends on the payroll.

The second was my relentless drive to win at all costs.

Of course, helping others and going all out to win are highly valued, socially approved behaviors. Plus, they reliably bring us and our families praise, status, influence, wealth, and more.

So where exactly is the problem?

Let's start with a man's impulse to rescue and save—to be perceived as everyone's favorite chisel-jawed hero.

Al-Anon conversations were teaching me that my stuckness around my business partner's dysfunction was rooted *not* in strength but in weakness—more specifically, in a shared dysfunction. The gravitational pull that locked us into the same orbit was an unspoken agreement: my role was to look the other way and make adjustments while wrapping myself in the mantle of "good guy to the rescue."

The payoff for my compromises was another day of peace—
or at least no fatal confrontations.

His role? Well, that was to skate free. That worked for
him because he could continue his intransigence and excessive drinking while everyone else paid the price.

An unequal, harmful relationship like this is called
"codependency."

An explanation of codependency I find helpful reads:
"Codependency is a behavioral condition in a relationship where one person enables another person's addiction, poor mental health, immaturity, irresponsibility,
or under-achievement. Among the core characteristics
of codependency is an excessive reliance on other people
for approval and a sense of identity."[13]

A simpler definition defines codependency as an over-
reaction to things, people, and so on, outside you, and an
underreaction to things, feelings, and so on, inside you.

Most decent people struggle to understand the line
between good and harm in this complicated dynamic.
I did. And if the word *codependency* still feels abstract
and squishy to you, let me tell you: facing its lock on
my relationships and decision-making process felt like
an appointment with death. (In fact, psychologists have
described a destructive, codependent relationship as a
"death spiral.")[14]

I felt humiliated to see the falseness and foolishness in
my "heroics" and to come to grips with my weakness and
my failure.

As Pia Mellody, author of several books on codependency, writes, the cost and the necessity of getting "sober" from codependence is made even more challenging because "unlike alcohol and drug abuse victims, codependents have often been rewarded for the inordinate amount of people-pleasing they engage in as a result of their disease."[15]

People pleaser? Yup, that was me. And my excruciating headaches had shown me that being a people pleaser didn't come free.

> "Unlike alcohol and drug abuse victims, codependents have often been rewarded for the inordinate amount of people-pleasing they engage in." -Pia Mellody

I asked my counselor to help me understand and work through my embarrassing stuckness. Through a series of difficult explorations, he helped me see how my nearly bottomless need to win admiration and approval from others, to be the rescuer who rides in on a white horse, had turned me into a compulsive people pleaser.

I had always found it very hard to say no to the requests and needs of others. I *wanted* to be a caring person, one who would always help and volunteer when needed. I selflessly served my church, my community organizations, charities, and individuals. I threw myself into running my business and caring for my wife and children, my aging parents, and—to tell the truth—my whole extended family.

What's more, the logic for my choices seemed airtight. Doesn't sacrificing for the good of others lie at the heart of Jesus's message? Isn't that what any good person is supposed to do?

I would give and give until I resented everything and everyone, including God. Then I felt guilty for my resentments. And God was to blame, wasn't he? After all, God was the one I had to work so hard to please, right?

It was a formula for disaster, and the formula cooked me good!

Even though I believed theologically and intellectually in grace, I operated by default programming that told me I was put on earth to perform for God.

Do you understand what I'm saying? If you grew up in the church, I guarantee you do.

how we get bent

I am living testimony to the profound blindness in which nice-guy-ness flourishes. Much of what passed for nobility was actually ego: I wanted to project an ethically and spiritually more elevated persona than the next guy.

> I would give and give until I resented everything and everyone, including God.

Clearly, I was just as in need of healing as the people in my recovery meetings were.

These insights came with an upside: I didn't need to feel like an interloper anymore at AA and Al-Anon!

My years of practicing codependency had left me unable to distinguish my true feelings from the expectations and needs of others and then respond with authenticity.

Maybe that's why my coach wanted me to ask myself five hundred times a day, "What am I feeling right now?" That was my path away from shaping my internal world and values by externals and toward authenticity.

You might be wondering where nice-guy dysfunctions come from.

Most of us learn in childhood to "cope"—which is to say ignore, numb, manage, or reinterpret reality. We do it to survive, but our relational instincts get bent in the process.

I had codependency modeled for me by my mother in her relationship with my father. He had grown up in a home where his father was rarely home because my grandfather worked as a traveling salesman during the Depression. When he did come home, he tended to let his temper loose.

My father was a good man—smart, visionary, hardworking, generous, and affectionate, a leader and a man of faith. But he was also critical, perfectionistic, and sometimes angry. Plus, he was the only one in our family who had "permission" to be angry. (He learned that from his father.)

When I was growing up, the unspoken rules were clear. My mother had permission to be happy, grateful, friendly, and respectful ... but not angry. Same applied to me. I had to stuff my anger. (Do you recognize the twin-star dynamic of codependence?)

I was afraid of stepping in the path of my father's wrath. So I developed my own internal radar to sense anger. I could smell it a mile away, and I would go into my self-protection and avoidance mode to get out of its path.

I'm thankful that, over the years, my father mellowed and grew spiritually and emotionally. And as I matured, a different kind of relationship became possible. By the time I was twenty-five, my father and I had become close friends. He referred to me as his "brother." I was forty-five when my father died. By then, I knew I had lost my best friend, and I knew that I had become his best friend.

Ours was a story of healing in spite of anger.

But I discovered that what happens later in your life doesn't change the programming from your childhood. Men I know who grew up in a home with an alcoholic or abusive parent, or where there was perfectionism and excessively high expectations, understand exactly what I'm talking about.

disappearing boundaries

In their powerful and popular book *Boundaries*, Christian psychologists Henry Cloud and John Townsend address the dilemma I experienced:

> Any confusion of responsibility and ownership in our lives is a problem of boundaries. Just as homeowners set physical boundary lines around their land, we need to set mental, physical, emotional, and spiritual boundaries around our lives to help us distinguish what is our responsibility and what isn't.[16]

When my daughter studied psychology in high school, she learned about dysfunctional people and dysfunctional families. Soon she was pointing out inconsistencies and imperfections in our family. My response to her at the time was, "Well, all families are dysfunctional; some are just more dysfunctional than others."

Of course, I wasn't being helpful so much as defensive while trying hard to keep a sense of humor about things. (She still loves to quote my "some are just more dysfunctional than others" opinion back to me!)

> My response to her at the time was, "Well, all families are dysfunctional; some are just more dysfunctional than others."

Children do not have the authority to enforce healthy boundaries. A child has to adapt and just try to avoid painful consequences. Any breaches of a child's experience of safety can create a psychic wound.

As adults, we carry that wounded six-year-old self inside of us, while on the outside we wear our confident grown-up persona. But our grown-up self continues to live out what we learned in childhood.

And that's what happened to me.

My poor boundaries were rooted in very deep-seated beliefs about who I was and who I was supposed to be. These beliefs had to do with duty, responsibility, and service to others. I thought I had to continually prove myself worthy with accomplishments. This resulted in a life of intense, seemingly nonstop activity.

Which brings up my second socially approved but personally costly behavior: my lifelong, all-out drive to win. As one of my daughters observed and declared to be our family motto, "Anything worth doing is worth overdoing!"

performance intoxication

Like most businessmen and professionals, I have a one-page personal business résumé that summarizes education and accomplishments. I also have a ten-page version. (Bet you do too.)

One day I read my extended résumé and just reading it started to give me a headache! True, I had accomplished a lot. But I saw that I had been reshaped by the process, and I didn't like what I saw.

I had become (as I related in the previous chapter) a "human doing" more than a "human being." Evidence for my socially accepted and highly rewarded compulsion stared up at me from my résumé: addiction to accomplishment and achievement.

I was a full-blown workaholic.

Evidence for my socially accepted and highly rewarded compulsion stared up at me from my résumé.

Like codependency, performance addiction can masquerade as an entirely good thing—the fuel in a hard-charging, success-oriented man. But as honest leaders and executives eventually discover, sacrificing everything to get to the top works only for a while. Eventually, it takes a heavy toll on our mental, physical, relational, and spiritual health.

We can end up losing the very pleasures and rewards we worked so hard to gain.

Very few addicts will readily admit or recognize their addiction. It might be the only disease that is accompanied by blindness to its existence.

Experts say a performance addiction is uniquely hard to recover from. For one thing, as with codependency, it delivers what one or both parties want most of the time. People come to depend on us *not* to require an equal, healthy relationship. For another, the success that results from our overwork brings nearly constant public and positive reinforcement—praise, recognition, awards, influence, status, and wealth.

> For racehorses like us, this payoff is as intoxicating as crack cocaine.

For racehorses like us, this payoff is as intoxicating as crack cocaine.

In his article "'Success Addicts' Choose Being Special over Being Happy," Arthur C. Brooks writes,

> For many people, success has addictive properties.... Praise stimulates the neurotransmitter dopamine, which is implicated in all addictive behaviors. (This is basically how social media keeps people hooked: Users get a dopamine hit from the "likes" generated by a post, keeping them coming back again and again, hour after miserable hour.)[17]

I don't mean to say that workaholics like us are somehow freaks of nature. Actually, most of us are born prewired for it. The great American psychologist William James once noted, "We are not only gregarious animals, liking to be in sight of our fellows, but we have an innate propensity to get ourselves noticed, and noticed favorably, by our kind."[18]

And success makes us attractive to others. (That is, until we ruin our marriages.)

Of course, the drive for success in and of itself is not a bad thing. In his article, Brooks compares it to wine: "Both can bring fun and sweetness to life. But both become tyrannical when they are a substitute for—instead of a complement to—the relationships and love that should be at the center of our lives."

what recovery looks like

My new life on sabbatical forced me to confront how my drive for success had been steering me toward pain and disaster. And as I explored the confusing mix of my genuine and false motivations, my counselor and I were able to untangle my codependent inclinations.

From there, we went to work to address the sick situation at the office.

He helped me hire a forensic accounting team. I brought in a consultant. I made another effort to lay out for my problematic team member a sensible, positive way forward. Really, it was one more chance for him to get into recovery or lose his job, even though he was sure I would never fire him.

He refused.

And I finally got the nerve to fire him.

With the rest of the team, we put together a plan, and the company did just fine. In fact, for the rest of the company, the absence of this miserable employee was like a breath of fresh air in the office.

Listen, I understand that there are no quick fixes for untangling habits of codependency and overwork. These are long-term projects that require change. In fact, I'll never become someone else (apologies to my dear *second* wife, kids, and coworkers).

> We can learn not to lose ourselves in the rescue of another or sacrifice our most important relationships in our dash for success.

I know from my own experience that, as healthy adults, if we keep at it, we can modify, limit, and redirect our compulsions. We can learn not to lose ourselves in the rescue of another or sacrifice our most important relationships in our dash for success.

In the next two chapters, we'll look more closely at the effects of childhood wounds and let what we find take us further into the mysteries of our subconscious so that we can become more self-aware.

Self-awareness doesn't bring instant results—all happiness and no problems. How I wish it did! Rather, it means that we choose every day to get honest about the pain our "bent" behaviors cause, then commit ourselves to an ongoing process of regaining what we've lost.

pause to reflect

1. Authors Cloud and Townsend define a boundary problem in relationships as "any confusion of responsibility and ownership in our lives." What relationships in your life might suffer in this way, and how?

2. What kind of relationship do you have with your drive for success? Allen uses words such as "fun," "tyrannical," and "attractive." How would you describe yours?

3. Have you ever experienced unconditional grace in a relationship or a group? What happened, and how did it affect you?

For more free resources, see

CHAPTER 5

crashing into
the past

*The secret to your recovery is to learn
to embrace your own history.*

—Pia Mellody

*I*HIT THE WALL WHEN I WAS FORTY-SEVEN YEARS OLD. That's when the tumorlike headaches knocked me off autopilot. I had to confront my choices in a new way in order to figure out why things had gone so wrong.

But that was not my first crash.

The first one occurred when I hit the ground in a spectacular plane crash when I was just twenty-two years old. At the time and for years after, that near tragedy made for one of my favorite adventure tales. (In dreams, it can still scare me half to death.)

The story always went something like this: *Fearless young pilot pulls off dangerous forced landing. In the dark. On a freeway. With a cargo of beloved friends and family. Thankfully, passengers walk away from the wreck unscathed and forever grateful to fearless young pilot.*

Now I see the story from an entirely different perspective.

Have you ever noticed that some of your most important personal stories change over time? Not so much in the facts about what happened but what those facts mean to you? What they say about you as a person, both then and now?

I would take it even further. The impulse to keep the deeper meanings of our life story hidden from ourselves is hardwired into every man I know. Including me.

At the same time, our history plays such a vital role in our lives that we could almost say *our past writes our present.* And this is especially true when we're talking about the wounds from that past.

In this chapter, I try to show from my family story what I mean.

owning what really happened

My father, L. Allen Morris Jr., grew up in Atlanta during the Great Depression and the family had very little of anything. His father, L. Allen "Jack" Morris, worked as a traveling salesman selling bolts of thread to the small general stores of the day. It was a hard life. Grandpa Jack was on the road for a week or two at a time and came home only for weekends—and then he was exhausted and mostly slept.

Jack was a good man, but he also had quite a temper. He would fly off the handle and frighten his wife and two kids with his hot temper. My father told me only a few stories about my Grandpa Jack. One that sticks in my memory is when my dad as a boy was trying to help his dad fix the screen door. Grandpa asked him to use the hammer while he held the nail. But Dad missed and squashed Grandpa's thumb.

Ouch!

Without hesitation, Grandpa Jack picked up his young son and angrily threw him off the front porch.

I guarantee the emotional pain from that rough treatment lasted longer than the pain from the hammer.

Of course, the burden of providing for his family during the Great Depression must have been overwhelming. It's difficult in today's world to imagine the awful specter of

> We could almost say *our past writes our present.*

hunger and want. When Jack's next-door neighbor lost his job, the man went out in his backyard and shot himself in the head, which happened a lot during the Depression, when men thought their life insurance was more valuable than their lives.

You better believe that bullet struck more than one person. Besides his family, it left a lasting mark on my grandfather, and, later, on my father too.

When my father graduated from Boys High School (now Midtown High School) in Atlanta in 1932, Grandpa Jack congratulated him, then told him he hoped he could get a college education. But Grandpa Jack had only a hundred dollars to help make that happen. So my father enrolled at Georgia Tech (an inexpensive state school at the time) and worked in a cotton mill and at other jobs to pay his own way.

When my dad was twenty years old, and still in college, Grandpa Jack died. At forty-eight, he had basically worked himself to death.

At that point, it fell on my father (who also went by Allen) to support his mother and younger sister. By then, my father had inherited a lot more than a family to support from Grandpa Jack. He owned a temper, a deep fear of failure, and an overpowering drive to succeed. Like many who grew up in the Great Depression, my father lived with a near certainty that the proverbial wolf was always at the door and guaranteed to leap for our throats again.

But he was determined never to let that happen. His mantra truly was that of Scarlett O'Hara in *Gone with the Wind*. You might remember the scene. She's been wandering the fields, sobbing, looking for something to eat. "As God is my witness," she cries, shaking her fist at the heavens, "as God is my witness—I'm *going* to live through this! And when it's all over, I'll *never* be hungry again!"

My father moved his family to Miami, Florida, a booming real estate mecca in the 1950s, and worked day and night to build a better life. And he succeeded. In time, he presided over a small real estate empire. He had the opportunity to partner with Arthur Vining Davis, founder of Aluminum Corporation of America (now Alcoa) and one of the richest men in America, to build the first regional shopping malls in Miami. He founded the Northside Bank of Miami and was named by the *Miami Herald* as one of the one hundred most important people in the first hundred years of Miami's history.

Like many who grew up in the Great Depression, my father lived with a near certainty that the proverbial wolf was always at the door.

Into this story, I arrived unexpectedly and late—I was born when my father was thirty-eight years old. By then, the family pattern was firmly in place. I, too, grew up in the shadow of a driven, hardworking, often absent father. I, too—without any conscious awareness of it—grew up feeling the hot breath of the wolf always ready to pounce.

When I was eight, my father had a heart attack. Thankfully, he recovered, but ever after, I harbored a secret dread that he would die suddenly, leaving the burden of family and business to me. And it scared me.

Like my father before me, I attended Georgia Tech. While I was there, I focused on one thing—not letting my father down. I felt I had to be ready at a moment's notice to step up. The only way I could see to do that was to learn everything I needed to know about business, real estate, and banking.

Only then could I pursue what *I* wanted to do and strike out on my own.

As my father approached sixty years old, he was eager to retire, and he had a plan in mind. One day when I was twenty-one and still a college junior, my father surprised me with his plan. "Allen, I want to make you president of one of our small real estate investment companies," he announced. "And I want to put you on the board of directors of the Allen Morris Company and the Northside Bank."

> President? Board member? That kind of talk made me feel like I had suddenly leap-frogged to the top of the heap.

When he said that, you know what happened? My own wishes instantly evaporated. I won't lie—the future he described looked pretty good.

President? Board member? That kind of talk made me feel like I had suddenly leapfrogged to the top of the heap.

I was still just a college student, with titles I didn't deserve, but with a mandate to learn fast and prove myself to older, wiser professionals. What I saw ahead was nearly limitless opportunity. What I missed entirely was the importance of confronting my family story and the unprocessed hurts that came with it.

Inner wounds from our fathers don't always come from being abandoned, or being called degrading names, or being hit or beaten with a belt, although those things have happened to many men I've known.

Father wounds are psychic injuries. They shape a child's interior world—his emotional makeup, self-identity, and survival instincts. Often the shaping is created by the intense pressure of spoken or unspoken demands, expectations, fears, or family values—and their influence is often generational. The emotional injury becomes an inheritance passed down intentionally or unintentionally—and often both—from father, to son, to grandson. (I'll share more about that in a minute.)

Trust me, as a twenty-one-year-old, I did not understand any of this. Who does at twenty-one?

"you don't want to see what's going to happen next"

While I was in college, I discovered that I absolutely *loved* flying—the freedom up there in the blue, the thrill of leaving earth behind to soar with eagles. It's a passion that's never faded.

I joined the Georgia Tech flying club, got my private pilot's license, and began flying on weekends.

In October 1974, I planned to fly a group of my friends from Atlanta to Houston for a fellow classmate's wedding. But first I had to fly to Miami (on Delta Air Lines) that morning to attend board meetings and executive committee meetings. That was my life now. A month before graduation—at just twenty-two—and I was already a company president and on multiple boards.

When I returned to Atlanta that evening, I loaded my six passengers, luggage, and wedding presents into our rented single-engine Piper Cherokee Six, and we took off at 11:00 p.m. to fly to Houston. I loved the beauty and smooth air of flying at night.

I'll admit, the risks and responsibilities all seemed normal to me. Acceptable. *Exciting.*

The crazy schedule? The crammed, late-night flight? Being the guy who made everything come together for everyone else? I'll admit, the risks and responsibilities all seemed normal to me. Acceptable. *Exciting.*

During flight training, I had repeatedly practiced how to handle the rare, but possible, crisis of engine failure in a single-engine plane. My instructor, Tom, would suddenly grab the throttle, cut the power, and say, "I've got the power. You've had an engine failure! What are you going to do now?!"

I would quickly run through my memorized emergency checklist:
- Full throttle.
- Full fuel mixture.
- Full prop pitch.
- Fuel boost pump on.

+ Switch fuel tanks.
+ Try restart.
+ Set the pitch down to seventy-two miles per hour for maximum glide distance and look for a place to land.

We practiced this over and over. One day I asked Tom, who had been an army pilot in Vietnam, "What do you do if you have an engine failure at night?"

He said, "You turn on your landing lights and look for a clearing to make your emergency landing."

"And what do you do if you can't see a clear area to land?"

"You're going to want to turn off your landing lights," he quipped.

He lost me there. "Why would I turn off my landing lights?" I asked.

"Because you don't want to see what's going to happen next."

> **"I am not afraid to die. I just don't want to be there when it happens!"** –*Woody Allen*

We both laughed (sick pilot humor). The conversation reminded me of the famous Woody Allen line, "I am not afraid to die. I just don't want to be there when it happens!"

As I completed the preflight checklist in the Piper, I remembered a maintenance problem in the plane that had surfaced the weekend before. But I had been assured that it had been repaired, so we proceeded to take off from Fulton County Airport into a clear moonlit night.

Since several of my passengers had never been in a private plane before, I pointed out how things worked, read the checklist out loud as I performed each item, and explained all the safety procedures and features. While we climbed above the dark, wooded neighborhoods of Atlanta, I pointed out the huge lighted parking lot below at Six Flags amusement park, a local landmark.

Then, as we climbed through four hundred feet altitude, the engine sputtered. And then it stopped dead.

Total silence.

this is not really happening

My first thought was, *No! This is not really happening! Not with six passengers on board, at night, at low altitude, over a wooded residential area!*

At four hundred feet of altitude and with the plane loaded to capacity, I knew I had about sixty seconds to make decisions and take actions. Then it would be over.

None of us knows in advance how we will respond in an emergency. Some will freeze. Some will scream and run in circles like Kevin in the movie *Home Alone*.

For me, everything became crystal clear. Each second seemed to stretch into a minute.

I went through each step in the checklist, but the engine would not restart.

Abandon restart. Focus on landing.

I did not have enough altitude to turn around and glide back to the Six Flags parking lot, much less to the airport. Below us, Interstate 20 stretched out in the darkness, but where?

Then I saw the headlights of a semitrailer, and behind it the headlights of a car. A plan clicked into place.

I set up my glide path to head for the black spot just behind the semi and the car. "We've got to make an emergency landing," I announced to the strangely quiet cabin. "Brace yourselves!"

In an airplane, your two friends are altitude and airspeed, but I was running out of both. I saw trees coming toward us and just beyond them the clearing for the highway. I pulled up slightly as the landing gear brushed through the leaves in the treetops and then I turned to line up my landing on the centerline of I-20. In the middle of my turn, a large green-and-white metal sign showed up directly ahead: "Exit Six Flags." I had to pull up.

That bled off precious airspeed. *Don't stall*, I told myself. That would pancake us into the ground. I pushed the nose of the plane down to regain airspeed and control, but by now I had to "play the ball where it lies," as they say on the golf course.

Right here was where we were going to land.

Here was a grassy clearing alongside the interstate highway. It had rained that day, and as soon as we touched down, the landing gear quickly sank into the mud, ripping the gear off. We skidded forward on the belly of the plane until we hit the end of a guardrail. The windshield exploded glass into the cabin, a fragment lodging in my left eyelid.

The plane wheeled around and slid sideways seventy feet along the guardrail until the shriek of metal on metal stopped. The rail had knifed into the left wing next to the fuselage. That was also the location of the left main fuel tank, which I had just filled with 100-octane aviation fuel.

Silence again.

In the first second after the plane came to rest, I thought, *Well, that did not go as I had planned!*

Then I switched back to emergency mode. Were my passengers okay? Was I? Now that I had a free second, should I call in a Mayday on my radio?

And then I smelled gasoline, and I knew I had to get everyone out *now*.

"Are you all right in the back?" I yelled. No answer.

"Are you all right in the back?" I yelled. No answer.

My best friend, Jim, was in the front seat next to me. He said he was okay but his feet were stuck in the twisted rudder pedals, probably where the guardrail had cut through the bottom of the plane.

"I've got to get the girls out of the back of the plane!" I yelled, but the cockpit door was on Jim's side, so I reached over him, opened the door, and climbed over him onto the right wing.

Standing on the wing, I saw my friend Ralph, the minister who was to perform the wedding we were going to in Houston, already out and sitting in the grass with his baby in his arms.

"Ralph, are you okay?"

"Yes, I'm fine."

"How's the baby?"

"He's fine. He just thought it was all part of the ride!" At least he'd kept a sense of humor.

"Great. I'll get the girls out!" I sounded calm, but I was in shock.

I stepped down off the wing to get around to the passenger door on the other side, but the moment I touched the ground, it felt like I had taken a bayonet in the spine. The pain was unbearable. As I lowered myself onto the grass, I felt the lower half of my body go numb.

The crash had broken my back.

Well, I hope there's no fire, I remember thinking, *because I'm not going anywhere.*

Thankfully, the passengers began clambering out and I realized that, against all odds, everyone was alive. Which didn't seem possible. None of it seemed possible.

How had I been able to climb out of the plane, anyway? Lying there on the grass, I couldn't remember.

And why was there no fire?

A metal fuselage sliding on top of a steel guardrail with all electrical systems on, and a hot engine, all bathed in 100-octane aviation gas? The plane with all of us in it should have exploded in a ball of fire.

But it didn't.

We only figured it out later. When the plane came to rest, the hot engine and electrical connections were on the uphill side of the guardrail and the fuel tanks were spilling on the downhill side of the guardrail, draining away from the airplane.

And we had all been spared.

happiness in a hospital

Fortunately, not many airplanes landed on I-20 that evening, so we got a lot of attention. Within minutes, an angel appeared to me wearing a Georgia State Trooper uniform. The trooper called in every emergency vehicle imaginable, including ambulances and fire trucks.

I'll never forget the looks of disbelief and even terror on the firemen's faces as they scrambled to hose down the fuel-soaked scene.

Everyone else survived that night with minor injuries. I, on the other hand, began a new life in intensive care and the surgical suite, where I underwent two spinal operations, each followed by body casts.

> Nothing worked. When they stuck needles in my legs and feet, I watched but couldn't feel a thing.

Unfortunately, the surgeries left me in intense pain and continuing paralysis. I remember the doctors asking me to wiggle my toes and not knowing what to think in my brain to make my toes move. Nothing worked. When they stuck needles in my legs and feet, I watched but couldn't feel a thing.

It was weird to feel like I was observing someone else's body.

The third surgery entailed more risks, but the doctors said I was young, and this was their best shot. They removed a rib along with a bone from my hip. Then they grafted the bone from my hip into my spinal column (called a spinal fusion), where injured discs had been removed.

Thankfully, that surgery was successful, but I still had a long recovery ahead of me. My new home became that hospital bed, where I was sealed tight in a body cast (my third by then), with tubes running out of my body.

Two months later, when I was still in that room in the same body cast, I had a revelation. It was Christmas Day. I was all alone, watching my favorite movies on the hospital room TV.

And I was happy.

In fact, I heard myself saying out loud to the empty room, "I think this is the best Christmas ever."

When I heard myself say this, I answered back, "What are you saying? You are one sick dude!"

I wondered about that conversation with myself for many years. At the time, I just knew I felt a powerful sense of relief. Nobody could expect anything of me. I didn't need to worry about disappointing anyone, especially my father.

It took me years to live into the fuller meaning of the story: I had been so obsessed with achieving and performing that a near-death experience, three surgeries, temporary paralysis, and months in a body cast *actually felt to me like I had been rescued.*

That's how much family weight I was carrying without knowing it!

But this would not become clear for me until after my *next* crash, the one I told you about in chapter 1. That one happened not in a private plane but in the painful, public collapse of my carefully constructed understandings about who Allen Morris was, why I did what I did, and how my father's and grandfather's stories had played a role in that crisis.

By then I was nearing fifty, spending every day down at the diner scribbling away in my journal.

the messages your father sent

"Every boy, in his journey to become a man, takes an arrow in the center of his heart, in the place of his strength," writes John Eldredge in *Wild at Heart*. "Because the wound is barely discussed and even more rarely healed, every man carries a wound. And the wound is nearly always given by his father."[19]

> "Every boy, in his journey to become a man, takes an arrow in the center of his heart, in the place of his strength." -John Eldredge

One thing I found in those pages of writing at the diner was an arrow in my heart. For years, I'd covered it over by saying, "This isn't really happening. Really, I'm fine."

In the 1991 dark comedy *City Slickers*, three unhappy friends in their forties decide to escape New York for a guys' trip to a dude ranch. In the safe space of their time together, they become vulnerable, and Billy Crystal's character, Mitch, asks his friend Ed, "What was the best day of your life?"

Ed describes his boyhood confrontation with his father. "I finally realized, he wasn't just cheating on my mother, he was cheating on us. So I told him, 'You lied to us. We don't love you. I'll take care of my mother and my sister. We don't need you anymore!'"

At that point, Ed's father turned around and left. "He never bothered us again. Well, I took care of my mother and my sister from that day on. That's my best day."

Their friend Phil asks, "What was your *worst* day?"

Replies Ed, "Same day."

That's a father wound. Yours may not be so obvious, but it's there.

We also receive wounds from our mothers, siblings, teachers, lovers, coworkers, and strangers. Looking into that heart wound, which we may have stuffed away so deeply we barely feel it anymore, can be painful and scary. But it is a necessary step to our healing. And that healing is our path to freedom and the power freedom brings.

My theme song has become "Desperado," by the Eagles. Don Henley sings,

> Your pain and your hunger, they're drivin' you home
> And freedom, oh freedom
> Well, that's just some people talkin'
> Your prison is walking
> Through this world all alone.

As a friend likes to say, "'Desperado'—performed by the Eagles, written by God."

The pain of an inherited message like "I am not enough" can take a man to the heights but it can also put him in a body cast. It can drive us to medicate our pain and confusion in ways that end up hurting us and those we love. We may not even be aware of what's happening until it's too late.

That is what the next chapter is about.

pause to reflect

1. What is the most important takeaway for you from this chapter?

2. We all grow up with, and then internalize, some kind of, "If you want to be okay, do/believe this ... or else!" message. What was yours? Who was the main spokesperson for it in your life?

3. How is that message from your past shaping your life today?

For more free resources, see

CHAPTER 6

journey into the shadow

*Until we know God, we cannot know ourselves, and
until we know ourselves, we cannot know God.*

—JOHN CALVIN

RECENTLY, I BACKED MY CAR OUT OF THE GARAGE. I know—talk about routine. Like you, I've completed that task by rote a thousand and more times in my life. Get in. Back out. Drive to work or the store.

This time, though, I was in a hurry. I checked the mirror, looked out the side window, and then stepped on the gas. Not too hard, but still. I had places to go.

And then I heard an awful sound.

A visitor had parked right behind me, dead center in my blind spot. Before I realized what was happening, I had raked the whole side of my car with the rear bumper of the other car.

How could I not see something so obvious as a car, and only ten feet away? How could something hidden create such massive damage so quickly, and without warning?

Answer: it was in my blind spot. The other car was right there, but I couldn't see it.

In this chapter I want to explore why most men go through life without seeing or understanding the part of us that drives so many behaviors. We'll discover that the truth was there all along, hiding in our blind spot—our subconscious mind.

In chapter 1, I introduced the idea of our "shadow," or "shadow self," a term coined by the Swiss psychiatrist Carl Jung to describe the part of our subconscious mind where we hide taboo or unwanted thoughts, memories, feelings, and desires.

Because in practical terms *subconscious* means "outside of our awareness," it's kind of a tricky thing to talk about.

Please be patient as we work through difficult concepts. We might need to think in new ways.

Also, doodles can help.

light and shadow (the doodle version)

For me, and for many of the men I've met at ALL IN forums and retreats, it is useful to visualize the relationship of our internal light and shadow with a diagram (see page 110):

Above the line represents the light of our conscious awareness. It stands for what we think we know about ourselves: our opinions, convictions, and beliefs. Jung and others tell us that the conscious part of our mind represents about 10 percent of the human intellect.

> Above the line, we find our convictions, beliefs, and commitments. The person and image we intend to be, and the one we try to project to others.

Below the line is the dark, or shadow, self, roughly our subconscious. The subconscious mind makes up 90 percent of our mental capacity. It's important to note that "shadow" does not equal "bad." It simply stands for the part of ourselves we do not see while it dominates our lives in so many ways.

In the next diagram, you'll notice a much thicker line separating the light from the shadow. It represents a wall that keeps us from seeing into our shadow.

Above the line—in the light of conscious awareness—we find our convictions, beliefs, and commitments. The person and image we intend to be, and the one we try to project to others.

But what about below the line?

In this dark interior space, we stuff all the fears, pain, and wounds from our past: unresolved and broken relationships, judgments, self-hatred, disappointments, injuries, abuse, and addictions. These parts of ourselves are not pretty; they are simply the truth about us.

Our shadow begins to form in childhood, before we're processing very much of our life consciously. As Franciscan teacher Richard Rohr explains,

> As children we learn which behaviors cause approval and disapproval from our family, teachers, and friends. If we want to have some sort of control over our lives and create pleasant outcomes, we tend to develop those things which are acceptable and repress those things which are not. Those things we repress or deny about ourselves become our shadow.[20]

Add to those the messages from our childhood of who we "should" be, what we "should" feel, whom we "should" love, whom we "should" hate, and what family secrets we "must" keep. All of it gets boxed up and stashed in our shadow self.

You can see why it gets so crowded in there in the dark. The diagram visualizes why the shadow can have such dominance in our lives.

But it's also worth noting that the wall of ignorance and denial between light and shadow can help us survive and thrive, at least for a time.

Some childhood wounds, for example, may have been so debilitating that our fragile selves needed protection. So the shadow, in effect, stepped in to help. Events were minimized, memories "forgotten" to the point that we judge they never happened or were "not really that bad after all."

Yet this "file it and forget about it" solution comes with an expiration date. It may have happened in the past, but we carry it with us every day, unseen but powerful. And one day what we have "forgotten" will start to work against us. The contents of our shadow will start to spill into our lives without our even knowing it.

Just to clarify: we commonly use *dark* or *darkness* to describe other experiences that shouldn't be confused with the shadow. We might talk about depression, grief, or a time of despair as being dark seasons. In our spiritual journey, we can feel lost to God and describe it as "a dark night of the soul."

But those are different experiences, even though pain originating in grief may lead us further into our shadow self.

understanding shadow work

Shadow work is the practice of proactively bringing our hidden parts into the light of consciousness in order to find healing. This may sound like a rather abstract goal, but shadow work has practical implications and brings immediate benefits.

The Shadow in Our Life

ill #1

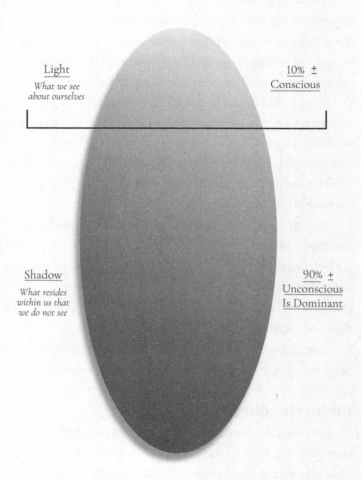

Light
*What we see
about ourselves*

10% ±
Conscious

Shadow
*What resides
within us that
we do not see*

90% ±
Unconscious
Is Dominant

"The Shadow Always Wins"

Even though "shadow" does not equal "bad," not being aware of its presence and influence limits our ability to free ourselves from its negative influences. "The less it is embodied in the individual's conscious life, the blacker and denser it is," Jung wrote. "[It] forms an unconscious snag, thwarting our most well-meant intentions."

That snag effect that Jung describes shows up in later life when we suddenly feel and behave in ways we don't understand or can't seem to control. As we noted earlier, "Until you make the unconscious conscious, it will direct your life and you will call it fate."

Which brings us to the promise of shadow work: in the light of awareness and acceptance, the shadow loses power to do harm, and we become able to harness its tremendous energy in positive ways.

In my case, I discovered that my insatiable drive to achieve and to prove my worth sprang in large part from a childhood father wound. Once I made the "unconscious conscious" in this area, I was better able to choose how to respond when seemingly preprogrammed unhelpful behaviors kicked in.

I was also better able to be kinder to myself in the process.

Of course, change of this magnitude can be extremely difficult. And the work is never finished until the day we die. But I know from personal experience that growing

> Even though "shadow" does not equal "bad," not being aware of its presence and influence limits our ability to free ourselves from its negative influences.

ill #2

The Power of the Shadow
Discovering the Shadow

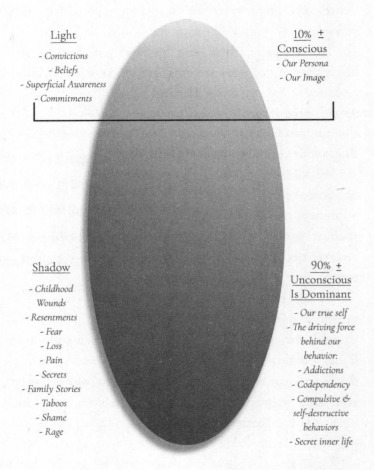

Light
- Convictions
- Beliefs
- Superficial Awareness
- Commitments

10% ±
Conscious
- Our Persona
- Our Image

Shadow
- Childhood Wounds
- Resentments
- Fear
- Loss
- Pain
- Secrets
- Family Stories
- Taboos
- Shame
- Rage

90% +
Unconscious
Is Dominant
- Our true self
- The driving force behind our behavior:
- Addictions
- Codependency
- Compulsive & self-destructive behaviors
- Secret inner life

"The Shadow Always Wins"

into the ability to choose yes or no to our own powerful impulses is a blessed freedom.

That's why, in our work with men, we see this journey of bringing light to our shadow as a kind of hero's journey— like the one described by mythologist extraordinaire Joseph Campbell. After all, a man is choosing at some level to take up the cause for those essential parts of himself that have languished for too long in the dark.

The journey of bringing awareness into our shadow, if we pursue it, continues through our lifetime. The third diagram visualizes this powerfully progressing awareness as stronger and wider beams of light that penetrate the shadow self to bring us greater conscious understanding of ourselves.

In this experience of "waking up" to the light, even rudimentary revelations can be profound and healing. For me, that has included seeing biblical teachings from a fresh perspective.

Consider: when the apostle Paul examined his heart, he noticed that parts of him were in conflict. "For in my inner being I delight in God's law; but I see another law at work in me, waging war against the law of my mind and making me a prisoner of the law of sin at work within me."[21]

Could this be a glimpse into a continual, ongoing struggle in his hidden shadow?

And then consider what Jesus taught about this inner world.

Jesus of Nazareth spoke about the light and the darkness within us and warned about the dangers of not being *ill #3*

Shining Light into Our Shadow
The Hidden Power of Our Shadow

Shining Light
into
the Shadow

Light

- *Convictions*
- *Beliefs*
- *Superficial Awareness*
- *Commitments*

10% ±
Conscious
- *Our Persona*
- *Our Image*

Shadow

- *Childhood*
  Wounds
- *Resentments*
- *Fear*
- *Loss*
- *Pain*
- *Secrets*
- *Family Stories*
- *Taboos*
- *Shame*
- *Rage*

90% ±
Unconscious
Is Dominant

- *Our true self*
- *The driving force*
  behind our
  behavior:
  - *Addictions*
  - *Codependency*
  - *Compulsive &*
  self-destructive
  behaviors
- *Secret inner life*

Exploring the shadow can be a sensitive process
and must be done in a safe environment
of grace, with a safe guide.

able to see ourselves for who we truly are. "If your eyes are healthy, your whole body will be full of light. But if your eyes are unhealthy, your whole body will be full of darkness," he said. "If then the light within you is darkness, how great is that darkness!"[22]

If we were to describe what Jesus is saying in Jungian terms, it might go like this: If my eye is "unhealthy," I won't be self-aware enough to see my very real shadow parts. And left unacknowledged, my blindness will actually expand its potential for harm.

different parts of the "operating system"

Meet Jeff, a successful entrepreneur and CEO for whom the journey into his blind spot brought not only healing, but an important spiritual awakening.

Throughout his life, Jeff seemed unable to sustain or find fulfillment in his relationships. When his second marriage was in a tailspin and he was struggling with depression and self-sabotaging behaviors, a friend recommended that he reach out to Cliff Berry, a counselor in Colorado who specializes in helping leaders in crisis. The counseling modality Cliff created is based in part on Jungian ideas of shadow work, described briefly here.

Later, Jeff said he thought of it more like "an internal valve job."

He signed up for a multiday intensive session with a goal of trying to figure out why relationships kept going wrong for him.

Here's how he described what happened next:

Cliff was able to help me see the different parts of my "operating system" to understand where, how, and why I was set up to fail in relationships. I began to see where, as a teenager, I had put up walls as a protection from a drill sergeant mother. I saw how, while I was getting my MBA, I had given away what was left of my heart to my father when he died. He had been my mentor and best friend. All of which made it impossible for me to be available, to any real depth or connection, in a relationship.

As Jeff did the hard work of bringing those wounds into his awareness and processing through them, he was able to bring the walls down and reopen his heart. He was able to grieve and make peace with the loss of his father and many other relationships to which he had become effectively numb.

Unexpectedly, Jeff also discovered a spiritual relationship he hadn't realized was possible. "In that depth of grief and process work," says Jeff, "I saw miracle after miracle unfold, giving me the experience that God was intimately, undeniably involved in my life."

God had always been involved, Jeff realized—he just didn't know it. He told me that during the intensive session he was able for the first time in his life "to experience a personal connection with God and his son, Jesus Christ."

No one was more surprised by that development than Jeff. He told me that his shadow work, along with the spiritual awakening that accompanied it, changed the trajectory of his life. He went from deeply depressed and hopeless to transformed and hopeful about the future.

"I was 'saved' in the biblical sense," Jeff says now.

The experience moved him so deeply that he became a certified coach and group facilitator of shadow work. He now leads others into what he calls "new, profound ways of breaking cycles and reclaiming who we are and who we are meant to be."

My takeaway from Jeff's story is that we *can* break free from patterns and submerged influences that have kept us stuck, no matter how strong they might be. We only harm ourselves and others more when we respond to our psychic pain like Scarlett O'Hara famously did in *Gone with the Wind*. You

> We *can* break free from patterns and submerged influences that have kept us stuck.

might remember the scene. Brought low by tragedy and loss (much of it self-created), watching as her man, Rhett, walks away for good, she sobs: "What am I going to do? I can't think about that right now. If I do, I'll go crazy. I'll think about that tomorrow ..."

None of us needs to stay stuck unless we choose to be.

what does shadow work look like?

Shadow work describes the process of exploring our unconscious self and bringing it to awareness. Typically the work is guided by a trained therapist or group facilitator (see more following), but a book like mine can, I trust, introduce you to this powerful healing path and motivate you to pursue it further.

Writer Kimberly Fosu explains shadow work in ways I find helpful. "Shadow work isn't a huge thing that requires years of planning," she says. "Shadow work is simply becoming aware of what's hidden and gradually healing those aspects of yourself."[23]

Fosu suggests four other ways we can become aware of the shadow in our lives.

Projection. When we see or assume something about others that's actually more about us than them, we are projecting. "We often project our shadows—our repressed anger, guilt, shame, and other things we don't like about ourselves—onto others," writes Fosu. "We lash out at people for the behaviors we don't like in ourselves."

> "We lash out at people for the behaviors we don't like in ourselves." -Kimberly Fosu

We can read these strong reactions to others as blinking lights that signal what we dislike or judge most harshly in ourselves.

Triggers. In the context of shadow work, a trigger is a reminder of past pain. You might feel unusually disturbed by a passing remark or notice that walking into your mother's kitchen tends to sink you in melancholy. But these experiences also lead us into our shadow, says Fosu. "The surface events that cause conflicts in our lives are not just triggers—they are messengers that enable us to become conscious of something that is buried deep within us."

Irritations that bring up outsize or misplaced emotional responses suggest that more is going on under the surface.

If we pay attention to these prompts, they can lead us toward healing. Being aware in advance also helps us make better choices in the moment.

Patterns. We all have emotions and compulsions that seem to play on repeat in our lives. These recurring experiences can lead us to our shadow. And they happen for a reason, Fosu says. "Patterns are expressions of the shadow because the shadow mirrors itself into your reality to be seen and integrated. The shadow wants you to become aware of it. It wants to be seen and accepted."

Because our shadow is largely in our blind spot, we need a trained guide to help us.

Compassion. Bringing tenderness and patience to this process is so critical. Most of us come fully equipped with the voice of a drill sergeant in our heads at all times. But that mentality just drives what's waiting to be revealed further back into the dark. "If you let the harsh inner critic come up and judge the shadow, you are rejecting it all over again and therefore making it bigger and stronger," advises Fosu.

Better to acknowledge and observe your discovery without judgment. "Observe it to understand it and then work to integrate it," she says.

One more important recommendation for successful shadow work is the following:

A trained guide. Because our shadow is largely in our blind spot, we need a trained guide to help us as an individual or in a group to navigate our journey into the shadow. Our ALL IN groups use trained facilitators and coaches.

How do you find the right person?

Ideally, you want to have a guide who is a certified shadow work facilitator or a qualified counselor or psychologist with experience in shadow work.

Second, you will want someone who is living in spiritual integrity and has a true accountability to a board of advisers. Seriously, check their references.

You might also consider a third safety step especially if you have concerns; ask a friend to observe your shadow work. Their goal is to make sure that the facilitator is truly serving you and not trying to manipulate you for his own purposes. (Can you tell I've been burned on this? More in chapter 8.)

luke skywalker goes into the dark

I will never forget the first time I saw the movie *Star Wars* in 1977. I was so captivated by it that I went back to the theater six times! I had never done that for any movie before. The stunning special effects, the dizzying space battles, the galaxy-sized drama seized my imagination.

Only later did I fully understand why.

In the second *Star Wars* movie, *The Empire Strikes Back,* Luke Skywalker seeks out the Jedi Master for his training to become a Jedi himself. His quest takes him to a strange new world. In a dark, foreboding swamp on the planet Dagobah, he encounters primal slithering creatures and an odd little green lump of a being. Slow to speak and spare with words, the being is not at all the mindless, mischievous critter he appears but Yoda, the great Jedi Master, in disguise.

Yoda teaches Luke about the power of the Force, a powerful energy field that remains clouded in mystery, just out of his mental and emotional grasp.

Soon, Luke feels drawn into a dark cave where he anticipates a confrontation. Luke asks Yoda, "What's in there?"

"Only what you take with you."

Luke grabs his lightsaber and blaster, but Master Yoda declares, "Your weapons you will not need."

"I'm not afraid!" Luke proclaims with youthful arrogance.

> Luke asks Yoda,
> "What's in there?"
> "Only what you take
> with you."

To which Yoda replies, "You *will* be. You *will* be."

On entering the cave, Luke confronts a vision of his mortal enemy, Darth Vader, and in the ensuing fight, Luke kills him with his lightsaber. But when the mask comes off, he makes a shocking discovery. The enemy he has defeated is not Darth Vader, but himself.

He is discovering that remaining ignorant of the self-destructive part of himself is the greatest threat to his well-being. Until that ignorance is unmasked, it will always lie in wait to destroy him.

With this newfound awareness of his own dark side, Luke can now connect to his true power, perhaps to become a Jedi Master himself.

Like our young hero Luke Skywalker, we can find freedom from our inner wounds and destructive behaviors only by traveling *into* and *through* and *beyond* our injured places and the pain and fears that come with them.

power in your inner being

In spiritual terms, I believe the deeper we go into our shadow, the closer we come in our experience of God. I would even say that *as we go deeper, God goes deeper with us.*

The apostle Paul wrote about our deep self when he prayed on behalf of his converts. He asked God to grant them "power through his Spirit in your *inner being,* so that Christ may *dwell in your hearts* through faith," and that they "may have power … to grasp how wide and long and high and deep is the love of Christ."[24]

Paul is imagining an interior universe as vast and varied as George Lucas's galaxy— and God everywhere in it.

I've often asked myself what Paul meant when he described God granting us power in the "inner being" and his Spirit dwelling in our "hearts."

I don't think he is talking about God's Spirit living in the right ventricle of our heart muscle or in our kidneys, as some cultures describe the metaphor of a person's inner being. I can't help thinking that Paul is imagining an interior universe as vast and varied as George Lucas's galaxy—and God everywhere in it.

If so, then our shadow is not an ugly, scary place where God's Spirit would never go. On the contrary, as we delve into the mystery of our own shadow, we can expect to find that God's Spirit is already there, understanding our wounds, our shame, our fears, and waiting for us and loving us more than we can imagine.

pause to reflect

1. Since the shadow represents the part of the self we can't see, how do you feel about trying to grasp something so elusive and difficult to understand? Do you find yourself hopeful? Doubtful? Resisting even going there? Why, do you think?

2. Allen quotes the astonishing promise of Jesus, "If your eyes are healthy, your whole body will be full of light." What does that insight mean to you? Where do you most need light today?

3. One promise of sobriety according to the Big Book of AA is that "we will suddenly realize the God is doing for us what we could not do ourselves." How might that be happening for you?

For more free resources, see

CHAPTER 7

when good men fall

*A man cannot become the ruler of his own
soul and genuine in his relationships until
he has been through some wounding.*

—ROBERT HICKS

SOMETHING HAPPENS TO MEN WHO HAVE FOLLOWED the rules and climbed the ladder to respectability and success. At a certain point, often between their forties and sixties, carrying the weight of their unexamined shadow becomes unbearable. Many people call this the midlife crisis.

I think of it like a beach ball.

When I was a boy growing up in Florida, a swimming pool was always nearby. A water game I mastered was called "hide the beach ball." I could hold a beach ball underwater for ages, a look of utter relaxation and innocence fixed firmly on my face. I learned to balance myself seal-like while sitting on it. I even pulled off holding two beach balls underwater at the same time.

When I tired, or just wanted to play a trick on somebody, I'd let go.

With an incredible *whoosh*, the ball would explode into the air, surprising and spraying water on anyone who happened to be nearby.

When we've been carrying a lifetime of unresolved pain, fear, guilt, or resentment, that burden can explode out of the dark in the same way. Earlier in our lives we were able to keep it repressed, but around midlife, what's hiding in our shadow spills out, shocking and often devastating those affected.

I'm talking primarily about what happens when a man's private struggle with anger or sexual fidelity suddenly breaks out into the open. Or in language of shadow work—what happens when we get stuck in our persona and remain blind to our shadow. The answer is that we become dangerous, hurting ourselves and those around us.

We have all seen this self-blindness play out. In recent years, numerous high-profile leaders in entertainment, business, and politics have been humiliated when their double lives were exposed.

Sadly, we've seen the same thing happen to well-known pastors and ministry leaders. In many ways, these are the most disheartening and damaging scandals of all. I think that's because we expect so much more of men who have made a career of serving God.

Trust me, I don't think of myself as better, more special, or less vulnerable than other men. (You'll learn more about that in the next chapter.)

The big picture, of course, is that *all men struggle with their private lives*. Good men. Bad men. Spiritually devoted men. Spiritually disinterested men.

All men struggle with their private lives. Good men. Bad men. Spiritually devoted men. Spiritually disinterested men.

Some of us are mostly winning that struggle and growing stronger. Others of us are mostly losing while we work hard to hide our downward spiral.

It's that simple.

Still, when the reputation and life's work of a high-profile friend of mine went down in flames, I felt gutted.

"it was you, a man like myself"

Conrad was a brilliant philosopher, teacher, and leader in the Christian community. He also led a global ministry that helped millions to know God. (Out of respect and compassion for him and those who loved him, I am not using his real name.)

My tie with Conrad was not a daily or intimate friendship, but it was not just casual either. I can count years of lunches, dinner meetings, and discussions together. I hosted his last public speaking event in Miami and studied at his apologetics center in England. I traveled internationally to assist and speak at his conferences. I made significant financial contributions to his ministry. I saw the great things he and his team were doing. I believed in him. I admired, loved, and trusted him.

Then, after his untimely death from cancer, it was discovered that Conrad had been carrying on secret sexual liaisons for years.

When I learned of it, I felt like I had been slugged in the stomach. I felt lied to and deceived and heartsick. I felt angry.

As more details surfaced about Conrad's secrets, I found myself thinking of King David's well-known lament in Psalm 55:

> *If an enemy were insulting me,*
> *   I could endure it. . . .*
> *But it is you, a man like myself,*
> *   my companion, my close friend,*
> *with whom I once enjoyed sweet fellowship*
> *   at the house of God.*

Can you feel the pain in those words? If you have experienced this kind of heartbreak or betrayal or been the cause of it for someone you love, you have a sense of what I'm talking about.

A friend of mine keeps a file in his desk drawer of promising leaders who fell victim to serious moral compromise. He calls it his "Burned List," and it's a long one. He keeps the list, not so he can feel holier-than-thou but as a warning to himself never to think he is immune.

> Because we live in the spotlight, we go to extremes to protect our public image.

It seems to me that leaders feel an unusual resistance to seeing or dealing with our shadows in this area. Because we live in the spotlight, we go to extremes to protect our public image. Which isn't us, of course—it's just our public persona, or social face we present to the world. Jung called it "a kind of mask, designed on the one hand to make a definite impression upon others, and on the other to conceal the true nature of the individual."[25]

Yet our work almost requires us to believe our mask *is* us.

Fr. Richard Rohr connects living in public while hiding from ourselves to shadow work. He writes,

> The more we have cultivated and protected a chosen persona, the more shadow work we will need to do. Therefore, we need to be especially careful of clinging to any idealized role or self-image, like that of minister, mother, doctor, nice person, professor, moral believer,

or president of this or that. These are huge personas to live up to, and they trap many people in lifelong delusion that the role is who they are or who they are only allowed to be.[26]

I found myself confused and wondering, *How hard was it for Conrad to maintain his persona and hide this compartmentalized part of his life?* What persona have I cultivated for myself? This led to more questions.

wrestling with giants

After my recent shock about Conrad, I found myself wrestling with five giant questions:

1. Can anyone trust *anyone?*
2. How could he be so deep in his deception and still . . . ?
3. Are there more hypocrites in church (or does it just seem like it)?
4. How can men learn to be more transparent?
5. If we are bystanders to a deception and want to help, what does "help" look like?

I would like to engage with each of these questions, drawing on my own experience and what I've learned from other men.

question 1: can anyone trust *anyone?*

Certainly, yes, for many things. But I no longer expect complete transparency from anyone. I've come to believe that all men fear being "found out." We carry this primal fear that we're frauds, or not good enough, and therefore always at risk of being disrespected or rejected. Which would feel the same as being destroyed.

So on matters where we feel most vulnerable—money, sex, reputation, and control, for starters—we tend to lie to others, or slant our words, or maintain a covering of silence for our own protection. More disturbingly, we lie to ourselves and rationalize and excuse ourselves for our moral failures.

As Rick Warren says, we "rationalize" our behavior, which means we believe our "rational lies."[27]

One insightful friend confided to me with a laugh, "When I tell the truth, it's usually by accident!" Sounds horrible, but I get it. Over the years, I've come to appreciate how rare it is to hear unvarnished truth.

> We "rationalize" our behavior, which means we believe our "rational lies." -Rick Warren

I don't think I'm being cynical, just compassionate about the reality of fear and weakness in the human experience. You'd be hard-pressed to find a thoughtful man who would argue with the prophet Jeremiah's bleak conclusion: "The heart is deceitful above all things, and desperately wicked; who can know it?"[28]

I'm reminded of the mayor in the movie *Chocolat*, starring Johnny Depp and Juliette Binoche. The strait-laced mayor of the little village, played by Alfred Molina, is a good and devout man. He is struggling to be faithful in his Lenten fast when he is overcome with desire for the delicacies on display in the local chocolate shop. So he breaks in. Early Easter Sunday morning, the shop owner, played by Binoche, finds him passed out in a sugar coma from his secret chocolate orgy the night before.

Having been judged and cast out by others, her response is to lovingly help the mayor recover, silently clean up the destruction, and generously keep his faithlessness a secret. She is nonjudgmental acceptance and grace personified. She is under no illusion that men under pressure can always be trusted.

They are human, after all.

Which brings me back to my opening question: *Can anyone trust anyone?*

Well, I think we can trust ourselves and others to be afraid, defensive, and flawed. And sometimes by grace to prevail.

> When men surround themselves with safe, grace-filled, confidential relationships, they will take enormous risks to own up to the messy truth about themselves.

I know this is true because I've seen that when men surround themselves with safe, grace-filled, confidential relationships, they will take enormous risks to own up to the messy truth about themselves, receive the same from others, and begin to flourish in integrity. (We look at the phenomenon of how men find transformation in chapter 9.)

These men are my real heroes—flawed for sure, and afraid, but willing to step into their fear around their secrets in order to become authentic and, yes, trustworthy.

question 2: how could he be so deep in his deception and still ... ?

You and I could complete that question in a dozen ways. In politics and business, we might ask the question, *How could he convey such conviction, integrity, and leadership in public yet be another person entirely in private?*

In a ministry context, the most common version of the question is probably, *How could he be so deep in his deception yet preach and teach so clearly and powerfully, and serve others so passionately?*

As humans, we seem able to operate from several versions of our self on any given day. And the more the shadow remains unexamined, the easier it is for us to do something with the left hand that the right hand is barely conscious of. It's called compartmentalization.

I have to believe my friend Conrad lived in horrible internal conflict about his corrosive secret, feeling more and more trapped. Imagine his private roller coaster: asking for and maybe feeling that he received God's forgiveness, then relapsing in his sexual violations, then not knowing why he couldn't control it, then maybe rationalizing his life as God's "broken servant" while desperately working all the harder to keep things secret.

Convinced he could never tell anyone the truth, could Conrad have believed that death was his only escape? According to the *Washington Post*, Conrad admitted as much in an email he wrote to one of the women with whom he'd been involved, "If you betray me, I will have no option but to bid this world goodbye. I promise."

My experience in leadership tells me that not every man who strays feels this kind of intense, internal conflict over their immoral or unethical behavior. I see two kinds of secret keepers: the charlatan or con man, and the good man.

the con man behaving naturally

Some men who aspire to leadership have no intention of living in integrity. They simply crave acclaim, power, influence, and wealth. We see these fakers exposed in every arena—politics, business, sports, religion, entertainment and the arts, science, and the professions.

What looks like a freer life is actually just a larger jail cell.

Steve Martin played a classic charlatan as Rev. Jonas Nightingale in the 1992 movie *Leap of Faith*. He explained himself to his partner, "I give my people a good show. Manipulators are sneaky. I am obvious." He had no illusions, or values, and he was not an obviously tortured soul. He was simply a con man.

We see charlatans typecast as villains in many movies and TV shows. Their main concerns are how far they can go and how long they can get away with it.

But what looks like a freer life is actually just a larger jail cell. According to the Big Book of AA, there's only one kind of alcoholic who's beyond hope: the one "who is constitutionally incapable of telling the truth."

the good man behaving badly

What about men who sincerely aspire to be great and good yet make destructive choices? We've all been there. Sometimes we go on making those destructive choices for a long time because we're angry or stubborn or just plain selfish. That decent mayor who succumbed to temptation, for example. As the apostle Paul wrote, "All have sinned and fall short of the glory of God."[29]

What about men who feel called to a higher purpose but find themselves crippled by a secret addiction?

Our definition of addiction, remember, is any behavior we can't seem to stop, even though we know we are hurting ourselves and those we love. In the language of AA, when we're addicted, we're sick, not bad.

It's hard for me to put an addict in the same category as the charlatan and con artist. I have known many men— some personally and some only by reputation—who have suffered terribly from substance and behavioral addictions. Thankfully, many have faced their need for change and gotten help. Many others, like Conrad, keep their struggles private only to bring more suffering in the long run.

But is there really a difference—in terms of the harm done—between a person who knowingly and carelessly uses someone else and a leader who genuinely cares for people yet ends up morally compromising himself and others?

Conrad wounded legions of trusting people who had benefited from his ministry, and Scripture teaches that those who aspire to become teachers will incur a greater judgment from God.[30] He may have excused his actions because of a distorted sense of religious authority. But innocent people were still devastated.

> Both the con man and the "good man" who make terrible choices are tortured souls, just in different ways.

We are all accountable for the legal and ethical consequences of our failures. Both the con man and the "good man" who make terrible choices are tortured souls, just in different ways.

But only God knows the heart, and he is the ultimate wise judge, not us.

question 3: are there more hypocrites in church (or does it just seem like it)?

Religious settings prime most of us for pseudo-honesty; the biblical term for that is *hypocrisy*, because the risk of real honesty is just too great. Unfortunately, a judgmental culture can keep a person or a whole community from the possibility of healing and change. The word *hypocrite*, as you may know, comes from the Greek word *hypo-crisis*, meaning playacting. So all our favorite actors and celebrities are hypocrites!

Of course, ministers—and good leaders of all varieties—*want* to help others. There are plenty of men and women who sincerely desire to be faithful, inspiring examples to others and may be brilliant, talented, sincerely compassionate, and giving. But some traditions require their pastors and priests to be saintly, pure, and pious. Especially in the arena of sexuality. Says Rohr, "They must maintain this impossible standard of an asexual man who does not see, feel or need human sexuality—even though we have been designed from birth to be sexual beings."[31]

I know of one church that was asked to allow a recovery group to meet in a separate building on their property. The leaders of the church balked but eventually had no problem with an Alcoholics Anonymous group meeting. When it came to a Sex Addicts Anonymous (SAA) meeting, though, the answer was a firm no. The prospect was just too disturbing and probably scary to them. The ironic part was that because the group practiced confidentiality, the leaders didn't know that several members of the SAA group who were getting help and healing were leaders in their own church.

> The church was not a safe place for its own leadership, much less for members and visitors.

Which suggests that the church was not a safe place for its own leadership, much less for members and visitors.

Does it have to be that way?

In contemporary times, I think of Brennan Manning, the beautifully honest author of many books on the grace of

God, including *The Ragamuffin Gospel*. He became an alcoholic after entering the priesthood and struggled constantly
with relapse. Yet he traveled widely and wrote extensively,
openly sharing his struggle in a powerful speaking ministry
in churches and on college campuses.

Thankfully, more and more religious and secular groups
understand that creating safety is as important as teaching
truth—and that this is the path to freedom and healing.

And in this transformation, often it is men's groups
that are leading the way.

question 4: how can a man learn to be more transparent?

The greatest barrier to authenticity is our fear. Our fears are
the reasons we create carefully crafted personas. A persona
is a mask or facade—a false but preferred self that we show
to the world around us. But the mask comes with a cost.

When I was a teenager, my uncle Johnny Houser was
the editor of *Variety* magazine in Hollywood. His best
friends were famous actors such as John Wayne and struggling young hopefuls such as Clint Eastwood.

Whenever I discovered a new heartthrob on the screen,
I would call my older cousins in Hollywood for the inside
scoop. Too often, the beautiful starlet or leading man was
a mess with a horrible life story. In Hollywood, there was a
saying: "Celebrity is a mask that eats away your face."

When you wear a mask long enough, you forget who
you really are. In a culture where appearances count for so

much, and the thought of transparency strikes fear, we can all lose our authentic selves, even to ourselves.

I wrestle with question 4 because I firmly believe that committing to transparency and authenticity in key relationships is the best way for leaders to stay off the "Burned List."

I've noticed two kinds of transparency: internal and external.

Internal transparency means you know you have nothing serious to hide because you are not knowingly carrying hurtful, destructive secrets. It doesn't mean the secrets are not there. They are. You are just not yet consciously aware of all of your secrets. That takes a lifetime of work.

> In Hollywood,
> there was a saying:
> "Celebrity is a mask that
> eats away your face."

External transparency means you live honestly and wisely in relationships. Of course, different relationships call for different layers of self-disclosure: shallow transparency with acquaintances, revealing transparency with close friends, and intimate transparency with our closest confidants who are committed along with us to authenticity and confidentiality.

To be transparent, we don't need to wear a cellophane suit to the office, but we do need some person or group with whom we can be "all in"—a confidential community where we can take risks to learn honestly about the parts of ourselves we hate, the parts that are making us sick emotionally and physically.

The apostle James linked confession directly with well-being. He advised, "Confess your sins to each other and pray for each other *so that you may be healed*."[32] When we choose instead to keep our secrets and look good on the outside, we begin to rot inside and accelerate our own decline.

Transparency in a group of loyal, like-minded, tightly knit fellow travelers takes healing to a whole new level. If you've found yourself in such a group, you know what I'm talking about. The incredible promise of honesty within a circle of radical safety and brotherly loyalty lies at the heart of our ALL IN forums and retreats.

Emotional safety allows men to dig deep into their stories.

(Don't miss chapter 9, "Circle of Trust," where we explore how authenticity can become a lived practice.)

Emotional safety allows men to dig deep into their stories with all the feelings, fears, and motivations associated with them. It allows others on the same journey to gently call them on their blindness and self-ishness and—if they are willing—hold them accountable.

That is the power of transparency.

When it happens, I have seen healing come in men's lives very quickly. I have seen distraught, defeated men release their secrets and find joy. I have seen angry men release their secret rage and find peace.

They start to become men of deeper integrity. Safe with themselves. Safe with others.

question 5: what does help look like?

If you're bravely reading through this chapter but find your own story of faithlessness or compromise being told, I want to encourage you. Whatever happened in the past, is happening now, or may be about to happen, you are not alone. You are not a failure. Most men I know, myself included, feel like failures on sexual matters. My strong encouragement to you is to find the help you need. A counselor, pastor, or wise friend is nearby. I encourage you to reach out.

But what if it's not you but a friend or colleague who appears to be courting disaster? Realistically, how can you help?

This is a tough one. When a man is bound and determined on hurtful and self-destructive behavior, his friends can advise and encourage. They can even intervene. But only he can open his heart to change.

Sometimes the most important thing that others can do is to continue creating an extraordinarily safe space and reaching out until he is ready to listen and ready to tell his truth.

I have been there—on the one hand, acting out of my own self-destructive hardheadedness, and on other occasions, patiently loving another man who is creating a world of hurt for himself.

Key words in both cases? Patience. Respect. Confidentiality. Persistence. Truth-telling. Restoration.

I so wish my friend, the ministry leader, had found his way to a welcoming circle of flawed and honest men, where he could have safely unburdened himself of his full, ugly story and started on his way to healing, both for himself and others. He would have spared himself and others a world of hurt.

leaders who fall (and get up)

King David of ancient Hebrew history was described in the Bible as a man after God's own heart. A high-profile hero. Bigger than life. He was acclaimed by God but not because he was perfect or without fault. He made some absolutely terrible decisions. His adultery with Bathsheba, for example, and arranging the death of her husband. But when he was confronted with the truth, he humbled himself and worked toward restoration.

Later, he wrote, "Behold, You desire truth in the innermost being, and in the hidden part You will make me know wisdom."[33]

His willingness to go all in—to risk searching his own heart and be truthful about his horrible violations—was the necessary beginning of David's journey to seek forgiveness and make amends.

That's when David could start to become a *real* hero—a man in touch with God and himself.

You can see it in the classic poetry, songs, and prayers he wrote in the book of Psalms, especially Psalms 19, 51, and 139. These psalms are a beautiful expression of his recovery, his freedom, his spark of creativity, his power, and his joy.

We all stumble and fall.

We all blow it.

But no one is beyond redemption. We don't have to let our failures define us. We have the power to write a new end of our own story.

Solomon said that "a righteous [good] man falls seven times [again and again]," and yet the Lord lifts him up.[34]

Any man who falls can also get up. But what good can come from a leader's fall?

As painful as it is to see good men go down in flames, it can open the door for *all of us* to look into our own inner life and, with the help of others, see a bit of our own authentic truth. Maybe that's why the Bible gives us the unvarnished story of fallen leaders. We see that no one is immune from spectacular moral failings. But we see, too, that no one has to stay down when they fall.

Maybe the fallen leader has actually given us a gift. Maybe he gave us a gift in his "death" and disclosure. A gift he could not give us in his secret life: the inspiration for us to start being more deeply honest with ourselves and with others and to reach for help sooner rather than later.

> Maybe the fallen leader has actually given us a gift...the inspiration for us to start being more deeply honest with ourselves and with others and to reach for help sooner rather than later.

When we embrace that deeper journey into the truth of our own lives, we can become the "wounded healer" that famous author and theologian Henri Nouwen spoke of so eloquently.[35] As leaders, executives, priests, ministers, rabbis, and teachers, we can then lead others to discover the kind of freedom and deep inner healing that come only from facing down our darkest demons.

This, I believe, using the words of one of my mentors, Francis Schaeffer, is "true spirituality."

pause to reflect

1. As you were reading this chapter, what *emotion* or *worry* were you feeling most strongly? Can you describe the feeling and its source?

2. What action is your feeling or worry prompting you to take?

3. If you are most powerful where you have been most wounded, how could you draw more intentionally on your personal hurts and failures to help others?

For more free resources, see

CHAPTER 8

breaking free from toxic emotions

The superior man leans into his fear.

—DAVID DEIDA

I HAVE COME TO BELIEVE THAT THE POINT OF OUR greatest pain and deepest wound is like an X on the treasure map of our lives. When that pain cries out, it is crying "Dig here!" This is where our greatest personal treasure is buried. This is the wound that, once embraced, has the potential to release our greatest personal freedom and the power to live more authentically.

In my story, I can take you right to the X.

My first wife and I were going through a tough season— really tough. In retrospect, we can both see that we were fighting our own private battles more than each other. For some time, she had struggled with childhood trauma and depression. Meanwhile, I had been sacrificing myself and my marriage to my achievement obsession.

I was committed to the marriage. But in her own deep pain, my wife said she wasn't sure she still loved me and didn't want to be married anymore.

When we decided to go for couples therapy, the counselor (I'll call him Eric), who had been coaching me for two years, seemed like a natural choice. I trusted him implicitly by then.

So we dove in.

From the start, I felt sure we were in good hands. Eric listened well, asked terrific questions, and brought incredible wisdom to our conversations. Over the many hours my wife and I spent baring our souls to each other and to Eric, the three of us became close. By then I thought of Eric as more than a clinician. In addition to being my personal coach, he was my spiritual director and confidant. I thought of him as my best friend.

And now he was an ally in our marriage.

When Eric suggested that my wife would benefit from individual sessions with him, and she agreed, I was elated. To me it was a sign of real progress and a reason to hope for her healing and our future together. We continued couples therapy, too, but Eric also invited my wife to accompany him on regular wilderness treks and to retreats and consultations—treatment he described as "critical" for her continued healing.

I consented. She still wasn't sure she loved me, she said, but I wanted to believe the best. By letting her go, I thought I might get her back.

> I saw the situation as a betrayal of biblical proportions, with me as the innocent victim.

(Do you remember the word *codependent?*)

Before long, I noticed a shift. More and more of my wife's attention became focused on her personal work with Eric. Less and less on us. When I voiced concerns that they were becoming too close, they both denied anything of the sort.

But they did get too close. I'll cut to the end of the story.

My trusted "friend," who was also our marriage counselor, manipulated my wife into an unethical and illegal romantic relationship that made a lie of what I thought we were doing to save the marriage. We were both the victims of his unconscionable manipulation and betrayal.

When the whole sorry mess came to light, I was destroyed. I saw the situation as a betrayal of biblical proportions, with me as the innocent victim.

Ugliness ensued.

In a fit of anger and pain I did the unthinkable, violating my own life values. I entered into a dark season of self-destructive indulgence that hurt others and myself.

My wife and I both did and said things we deeply regret. We learned firsthand that "hurt people hurt people." In my hurt, I hurt many others, which I wish I could change but I could not undo. And though we tried to patch things up, we never could. A few years later, our twenty-eight-year marriage ended.

> If we fail to make that connection between old wounds and intense emotion now, these powerful feelings can drive our lives in ways we will come to regret.

I have suffered excruciating pain in my life: concussions, broken bones, broken teeth, torn meniscus, cancer, the broken back I told you about, and multiple surgeries, but nothing compares to the pain of a broken heart.

Maybe you've been there.

When I ask guys to identify their own big, unmistakable X, a majority go straightaway to abuse, abandonment, or betrayal in love. Men don't feel their feelings? Don't you believe it! On matters of the heart, the wounds go deep.

The X on my treasure map was the childhood wound of abandonment. When my wife pulled away, I understandably felt abandoned, but in response I, too, pulled away. Bad move. (My wound did not, by the way, mean that my parents had *literally* abandoned me when I was fourteen by sending me to a distant military school—*but that's what it felt like to me.*)

In this chapter we look at a familiar list of powerful, negative emotions—most often rooted in our particular wounding—that can hijack our lives, especially when we're slammed by relationship crises.

Anger. Resentment. Fear. Shame.

These four consistently show up as big problems for most men I know, me included.

You know now that much of the time this is our shadow revealing itself. And if we fail to make that connection between old wounds and intense emotion now, these powerful feelings can drive our lives in ways we will come to regret.

It's no wonder that thousands of books have been written to address these emotions.

To remind you, I don't speak as a credentialed psychologist but as a bruised and battered, wiser-than-he-used-to-be fellow traveler who cares a lot. I run a men's program with retreats to provide men with a safe environment to explore their inner selves. If you need professional help, or someone who loves you believes you do, do yourself a favor—reach out.

that little thing about poison: resentment

The Big Book of AA calls resentment a *spiritual* malady and "the offender that destroys more alcoholics than anything else." For any of us, resentments can drive all sorts of escapist, self-medicating choices and seep into how we do life.

Alcoholics in recovery taught me an important lesson on this. They learn to recognize resentment as a kind of early warning system for falling off the wagon. Hold on to your resentments—let that sweet misery roll around in your heart—and you'll be picking up a drink soon.

There's a perverse logic in hanging on to what's causing us suffering. It's been said that holding resentment toward someone is like drinking poison and waiting for the other person to die.

> Holding resentment toward someone is like drinking poison and waiting for the other person to die.

I know from personal experience that this is right. I'm never more miserable than when I'm in the grip of a big fat grudge. And I'm never more likely to make those around me miserable too.

It's also true that even when we don't consciously feel our resentment, or notice its effects, others often do.

A friend of mine was brutally dominated by his intense and controlling father. His father's domination extended from his childhood into his adult years. Sadly, that made for a lot of rot. Even today, my friend's unhealed father wound affects his own personal and business relationships. By the numbers, he still looks pretty good, but colleagues experience him as defensive and emotionally closed off. Stunted in his professional growth. Successful, but not terribly happy.

He seems unable or unwilling to connect the pain surrounding the original hurt with how his life is going now. A barrier looms between the two experiences. In my opinion, he would be ten times more successful if he would face and release the resentment he carries toward his father.

As damaging as unresolved resentments can be, letting go of them can feel like being set free.

Meet David, former president of an $80 million company, who discovered he needed to let go of buried resentment. He had stepped out of a C-suite position to launch a consulting business of his own, only to find himself in a losing battle with

The negative emotions were now sabotaging his ability to excel in his new venture.

anger and resentment toward his father. The X on his life, he realized, related to extreme verbal abuse from his father when David was eleven years old.

The pain from that terrible experience had put a blight on his relationships and saddled him with shame, sadness, and self-blame. The negative emotions were now sabotaging his ability to excel in his new venture.

Eventually, the struggle led him to our men's ALL IN retreat on shadow work, where things changed for him in a big way.

"Sorting through my issues in that context," he said, "I had a moment of clarity forty years after that incident. I was able to see I no longer had to carry a burden given to me by my father. As a matter of fact, I realized it was never mine to carry. So I set it down.

"That decision changed my outlook," he told me. "The ball and chain fell off my ankle—and my heart. It's gone. I've thrown away the demonic lie of unworthiness that had been in my heart."

Which led to another aha! moment. He realized that the walls he had been putting up in his life were indiscriminate. "Those walls didn't care who they kept out," he explained. "A barrier to my dad had become a barrier to my wife. I was separating myself from my wife, my kids, even God in ways I didn't realize."

> "Those walls didn't care who they kept out...I was separating myself from my wife, my kids, even God in ways I didn't realize."

Since his breakthrough, David has experienced a renewed surge in energy and optimism. His consulting business is taking off. He's already earning twice what he did in the executive position at his prior company. And he says his stress level is a fraction of what it used to be, while his vocational satisfaction is off the charts.

He's particularly gratified to see the positive impact he's having now on others in his orbit.

your steaming pile of grievances: anger

If resentment is a kettle of hot water, then anger is the kettle at a hard boil. And anger—though it's often repressed—is the most common and powerful emotion I find in men.

I used to have a close relationship with Wyatt, a brilliant, talented CEO. Unfortunately, he couldn't seem to make his insides match his outsides. During a monthly meeting we were both part of, he felt compelled to dominate, focusing on his achievements but disconnected from his feelings. He never could say what he seemed so angry about.

At work, I noticed he took pride in berating underperforming employees. He used to complain to me about team members he didn't think were smart enough. And he wasn't into warm and fuzzy. He'd say, "If you want a pet, for God's sake buy a dog."

Closed to one emotion usually means closed to others. Maybe for that reason, he was not able or willing to open himself to authentic relationships.

> I seriously considered violence. And as a gun collector, hunter, and black belt, I had options.

I lost touch with Wyatt for several years, then recently heard tragic news. He had committed suicide. I was shocked and saddened, yet on reflection not entirely surprised. I believe it is likely that the pain he suppressed in his shadow became too much to bear.

It's a heartbreaking thought.

After my marriage blew up, I was furious and obsessed for a long time. Months. Okay, years. And I knew exactly what I wanted.

Revenge.

Justice.

Compensation.

To get it, I seriously considered violence. And as a gun collector, hunter, and black belt, I had options.

Fortunately, I didn't commit any capital crimes before I realized that my rageful wants could not be trusted. I was like a dog after it's been hit by a car, trying to bite myself and anyone else because of the pain.

I did pursue legal alternatives. Criminal charges were filed.

Did I have a right to feel angry? Hell, yes! But as I sat with my justified anger, I eventually asked myself if I was the only man in the history of the world to have been betrayed.

Well, no.

Maybe you know what it's like to feel betrayed.

Men throughout history have been betrayed in one way or another. Why did I think I was so special? As my furies cooled, something in me clicked. The story I had been telling myself began to change.

Ultimately, I became aware of deeper, more significant needs. I was faced with new questions:

+ *Do I want to live as a vengeful and hateful victim?*
+ *How long will I sacrifice my peace and well-being to my rage and resentment?*
+ *What could I learn about myself in all this?*

In both Jewish and Christian scriptures, we are told to put down the ledger of our grievances. "'Vengeance is Mine, I will repay,' says the Lord."[36]

Depending on how you think the world works, you might think of God's vengeance as karma—roughly, the idea that the universe "does back" to the bad guys what they "do unto you."

But increasingly, I see releasing to God my steaming ledger of grievances as a powerful principle for making peace and finding healing. I do believe God brings good out of evil. But now I read the "I will repay" pledge more as a divine invitation that can rescue individuals and nations from the ruinous cycle of victim-revenge-victim.

> "We are the heroes of our journey when we stop being the victims of our lives." -Joseph Campbell

As illustrated by the adage about drinking poison, if we hold on to our anger, blame, and unforgiveness, *we take unnecessary suffering on ourselves.* We are choosing to be the victim of that wrong all over again. Instead of choosing to be bitter, we can choose to let it make us better.

"We are the heroes of our journey," wrote acclaimed professor and author Joseph Campbell, "when we stop being the victims of our lives."[37]

unlearning disconnection

Since I grew up learning to be afraid of anger, I would often disconnect from anger—my own and that of others. A healthy man can own his anger in a clean way, aligned with his truth. And think of the power of the human rights movements through history to channel anger, bring clarity around injustice, and mobilize the public to take action.

On the other extreme, I've noticed that a high proportion of nice church folk, along with others who depend on tightly controlled, nonthreatening personas, seem to have mastered the art of living *without* anger. Even when an angry response is in order.

How do they do that?

I can tell you how.

At one retreat, our small group of men sat around a campfire. Our facilitator noticed that I had not responded to another person's highly disrespectful remark about me. When he asked me how I felt, I said I was not angry.

But he wasn't convinced. He asked me to pick up a large rock nearby. It felt like it weighed maybe twenty-five pounds, but ... no problem.

Then he invited me to stand outside the circle while he continued the main discussion. Fifteen minutes passed, and that rock gained a lot of weight. By now I wanted to sit down, so I asked if I could rejoin the group.

"No, that's all right," he said. "Please stay where you are."

Ten more minutes went by, the rock turned into a boulder, and every muscle in my body was screaming bloody murder.

I gasped, "I'm ready to rejoin the group now!"

Still, the facilitator ignored me, until I said the words: "Okay, now I'm really pissed. I'm not holding this damn rock anymore!"

And that was the moment I got in touch with the original violation. I *was* angry at the friend who was way out of line. My actual experience and my true feelings were finally aligned.

That's what it took for me to connect with my appropriate anger.

My disconnection from anger is an example of what's called dissociative behavior. Any psychologist will tell you that disconnection between an experience and an appropriate feeling about that experience is frequently associated with trauma or other formative wounds in childhood.

> When I was growing up, it wasn't safe for me to express anger, so I learned to deny and repress it.

That was me. As you saw in chapter 4, when I was growing up, it wasn't safe for me to express anger, so I learned to deny and repress it. But it lived on in my shadow, limiting the range of emotions I could feel and, later, busting loose in outburst of anger.

pulling the thread: fear

You may have heard that anger is often an expression of our fears. This rings true to me.

For me it is like pulling that thread on a sweater. As I follow the thread of anger or resentment, it unravels all the way back to my basic fear. For me, it's the fear that I am not enough—not good enough, not smart enough, not fast enough, not strong enough.

For you, the thread might lead to fears of being violated, of being disrespected, of being left out or abandoned.

Remember that our anger and fear are often inherited—in other words, a fear that is not all yours. Maybe as a child we observed our parents' fear of financial failure or the pain of their financial failure. Or their fear of their loss of reputation. Or their fear for their safety. Or their experience of being disrespected or discriminated against.

I think of a primal wound as a formative disruption in childhood that leaves the child feeling that the original connection to the parent is threatened or has been cut off. It may become our life's motivating force—sometimes expressed defensively (as in the one thing we want to prove is *not* true about us).

But wherever it originates, anger comes bursting forth when a person gets poked in a primal wound. At the time, the rageful response can seem far out of proportion to the offense.

You may say, as I did, "But I'm not angry." Instead of expressing anger, I stuffed it, only to discover it doesn't go away. It's like swallowing a hand grenade.

We express our stuffed anger often in mindless behaviors, such as overeating and drinking, which "medicate" away our feelings. We don't "see it" until we gain fifty pounds or—as they say in AA—"keep breaking out in handcuffs."

Fortunately, in shadow work and other ways, we're often able to follow our anger to its source. This is the journey into our self-awareness. And with healing, a habitually angry man can learn to become a safe person. I know this is true because I saw it happen in my own father. By the time we were adults together, he had a better understanding of his repressed anger and its underlying fear. And our relationship blossomed as a result.

Next time you sense your anger about to erupt, pull the thread back to its beginning. That will help you unravel the tangle of your emotions. You can do this by asking yourself,

- *OK, I am really mad—so what am I afraid of?*
- *Am I afraid I am not smart enough?*
- *Am I afraid of a financial loss?*
- *Am I afraid of a loss of my reputation?*
- *Am I afraid that my family is not safe?*
- *Maybe, I am angry that someone didn't serve me in a store when I was next in line? So,*
- *Maybe, I feel disrespected or disregarded? So,*
- *Maybe, I am afraid that I am really not as important as I like to think I am? So,*
- *Maybe, I am not! So,*
- *Can I deal with that and accept that?*
- *Can I have a good laugh at myself for thinking I was so important?*

That's how I follow the thread to find the fear behind my anger. So far, I *always* find the fear. Then I'm able to see the truth about myself, decide if my anger is really appropriate, and choose a healing path.

For a long time, we may not understand where our unreasonable reaction of anger or rage is coming from. But we can continue to reach for our tools. Ask "What am I feeling now?," "Why?," and "Where might it be coming from?"

In so doing, we allow our shadow to be our teacher.

162 • all in

that awful slime: shame

The toxin of shame takes a heavy toll on men. It robs smart, talented, successful men of joy by telling them they are profoundly not okay. In the previous chapter, we looked at the ways misdirected or uncontrolled sexual desires can burden a man with shame and guilt.

Shame is different from guilt, though. We feel guilt when we believe we have *done* something bad. We experience shame when we believe we *are* bad. Shame is like the gunk that grows under a rock at the bottom of a stream. We feel sure that unless we keep it hidden, it will slime our lives.

> Shame is like the gunk that grows under a rock at the bottom of a stream. We feel sure that unless we keep it hidden, it will slime our lives.

But I've found the opposite to be true. When we keep it beneath the rock at the bottom of the stream (suppressed and out of sight), the threat is real. But when we pull it out, turn it over, and expose it to the sunlight, the shame slime dries up and blows away.

How do we expose the shame to the sunlight? One way is by sharing our humiliating belief or experience—real or perceived—with other men in a safe, confidential gathering. Bringing shame into the light helps us see the lies that have bound us.

And once we are living in the truth, new feelings will follow.

What usually pops out first is relief, then the return of joy, quickly followed by a new experience of freedom.

bold move, rick

Not long ago, I rewatched the 1942 Hollywood classic
Casablanca, a film set in Morocco in the early days of
World War II. My wife, June, a scriptwriter herself, tells
me *Casablanca* has been voted by scriptwriters as the best
movie script ever written.

You probably remember: the hero, Rick, played masterfully by Humphrey Bogart, prides himself on staying aloof
from war and violence all around. Though charming and
dapper, he has little sympathy for the problems of others,
often saying, "The only person I care
about is me." He's the picture of the
stoic, self-controlled man admired by
others and pursued by women.

Things change when his former
sweetheart Ilsa (Ingrid Bergman)
shows up in Rick's Café Américain.
Her presence brings back a flood of
memories, especially the pain of her abandoning him years
earlier. We realize that Rick isn't so much a stoic as a refugee,
hiding behind a wall of hurt, resentment, and anger.

> I've noticed that letting go of toxic emotions is not a onetime act. It is a process.

But when Rick decides to embrace and move past his
pain, he is able to help Ilsa and her husband escape the
Nazis. In that bold move, we sense that Rick is making his
own emotional escape.

I've noticed that letting go of toxic emotions is not a
onetime act. It is a process of peeling the onion of our inner
life only to discover as we go deeper that there is always one
more layer of truth.

"Peeling the Onion"
of Our Inner Life

———

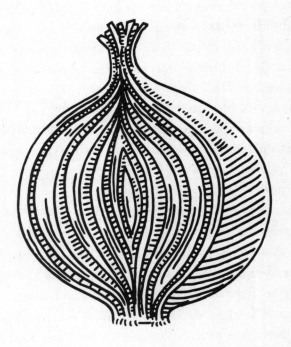

The infinite process of self-discovery.
When we achieve a milestone of self awareness,
we discover there is always one more layer revealed

Anger and grief from past wounds, especially intentionally inflicted, or malicious, wounds, rarely dissipate quickly and may return in waves over months and years. But I try to receive each new wave as an invitation to release these feelings again to God and thank him for his greater purpose in my life.

the grain of gratitude

A seminar leader I knew loved to tell the story of the painful irritation of a grain of sand. The grain of sand in our eye can cause a terrible, painful irritation, he explained. If it's not removed, it will cause inflammation and a bad infection and will eventually cause blindness.

That same grain of sand in an oyster will cause the same painful irritation. But the oyster secretes a smooth coating to soothe the irritation, which, over time, produces a pearl of great beauty and value.

When I experienced the engine failure in the rental airplane that left me temporarily paralyzed and permanently injured, I concluded that the rental company had missed an important maintenance step that contributed to the wreck.

I faced some choices.

I could blame and seek revenge. I could sue for justice and compensation. I could remain a victim.

Or I could direct my life energies to healing, to surviving the pain, and to learning to walk again. I could intentionally "squeeze the juice" out of the experience to learn what God might want to teach me through it.

When my first wife and my trusted friend betrayed and deceived me, I faced the same challenge, only this time it was even more wrenching: hold on to the rage, as I had every right to do, and suffer the effects of my own poison, or let go and choose life.

> I could remain a victim. Or I could direct my life energies to healing.

Both times, I faltered. I tried to let go, only to grab on to my grievances again. I tried again and again to forgive and move forward, only to double back into resentment, anger, blame, and victimhood.

Eventually, with the help of God and loyal, safe friends, I was able to choose the better path. And what a difference that has made in my life!

These days, the X on my life's treasure map triggers much less pain and a lot more gratitude.

If it had not been for my plane crash injury when I was a young man, I would have missed a great deal:

- Empathy for people suffering from long-term injury and disability. For example, I can embrace and appreciate the importance of accessibility design as a real estate developer.
- Humility to accept and live with my physical limitations.
- The greater urgency I feel now to use my limited time on earth for things that matter most.

If it had not been for the relationship breakdown that resulted in my divorce, I would have missed much as well:

- Empathy for so many others who suffer the pain of broken relationships.
- A new awareness of the gift of loyalty and the cost of betrayal. (Everyone is betrayed by someone, even Jesus by his close friend.)
- Greater intimacy with my children, who tell me I am more self-aware, present, and approachable.
- The opportunity years later to meet and marry my precious partner, best friend, and beautiful wife, June.

Like the grain of sand in the oyster, you and I can channel our energies toward transforming the losses and humiliations in our pasts into lives of great worth and beauty today.

pause to reflect

1. What would you say was the essential message of this chapter *for you*? Why?

2. Most men would rather take on a sword-wielding ninja than an intense, negative emotion such as fear or shame. Reflect on which strong negative emotion you are most likely *to avoid dealing with*. What simple steps could you take that would move you toward it with humility and courage?

3. Take another look at Allen's thoughts on gratitude. Are there very real wounds in your life that are waiting for the gift of your gratitude to turn them to strengths?

For more free resources, see

CHAPTER 9

circle of trust

*The strength of the pack is the wolf, and
the strength of the wolf is the pack.*

—RUDYARD KIPLING

*I*THOUGHT ABOUT TITLING THE CHAPTER "THE WAYS of the Tribe." But that might imply we're talking about those who favor fire dances and nose rings or the fashion these days of hanging out with those who believe what you believe in a narrowly defined window of political and spiritual views.

That's *not* what we're talking about.

This chapter is about survival!

It's just a fact that a leader's chances of avoiding a mid-career crash increase dramatically if he commits himself to authentic, truthful, vulnerable relationships with other men. Not just the outward appearance of it but the raw and visceral connection between teammates who understand they are on a life-or-death mission.

For most men I know, words such as *vulnerable* and even *relationships* do not roll easily off the tongue. Antennae go up. Helmet visors snap shut. We sense trouble closing in.

If you react with caution to the whole "men's group" idea as a solution to anything, I get it. My guess is you've suffered from being part of a men's group that failed you. You might have found yourself in a professional group that devolved into boasting about exploits in sports, sex, or business. That can be fun if you want to score points among your peers, but you leave thinking, *Yeah, that's not what I need.*

Or you have found yourself in an accountability group gone wrong. You came with a sincere need only to leave with an even heavier burden of judgment and shame.

You don't need that either.

But whatever your previous experience, I promise that walking away from your band of brothers is no solution either.

Psychologists, pastors, coaches, and sports trainers agree: a man who's committed to reaching peak perfor- mance is most likely to achieve it in the company of others striving for the same goal.

Harville Hendrix summarizes the matrix of hurt and healing when he says, "We are born in relationship, we are wounded in relationship, and we are healed in relationship."[38]

> **"We are born in relationship, we are wounded in relation- ship, and we are healed in relationship." -Harville Hendrix**

King Solomon was speaking for performance addicts everywhere, I believe, when he looked out on the stage of his life and saw "a man alone." But did that terrible insight—which we noted in chapter 1—lead one of the world's best-known wise guys to make a U-turn?

I'd like to think so. What he wrote three chapters later seems to be giving his former, loner self a talking-to:

> Two are better than one,
>> because they have a good return for their labor:
> If either of them falls down,
>> one can help the other up.
> But pity anyone who falls
>> and has no one to help them up....
> Though one may one be overpowered,
>> two can defend themselves.
> A cord of three strands is not quickly broken.[39]

I love that visual of the braided cord and the better outcome it suggests. It tells me that when I commit to telling the truth in a caring, bonded community, I put catastrophe on hold and find the power I seek. (In fact, the first group of young professionals I started after college was called "Our Cord Group.")

In my experience, the braided bond is the only thing that silences the lonely whine of the top dog.

a different kind of gathering

Early in my career, I was introduced to YPO Forum. As you may know, YPO is a global leadership community that sponsors multiple opportunities for men and women in leadership to grow personally and professionally. Their forum model offers a closed, confidential group of six to twelve company presidents who meet monthly and go away annually for a three- to four-day retreat.

I participated in three forums and benefited from each one. They were certainly better than anything I had experienced before in my working life. Yet over time, I became restless. The group's potential was regularly limited by a fear of vulnerability, conflicts of interest, even intentional sabotage.

Sabotage happens, for example, when one person is allowed to dominate or to steer the discussion off point. The saboteur may be determined to stroke his own ego or keep the group from going deeper because that feels threatening to him. When he succeeds, others in the group leave unsatisfied.

As far as I could tell, these outcomes didn't happen because no one cared. But after twelve years of "good" forums, I wanted something not just good but indispensable.

By then I had noticed another recurring phenomenon. In my work with executives in Miami—all of them talented, well-motivated high achievers—I saw good men "hitting a wall" in their personal and spiritual growth. They started out well, growing in their faith and influence, only to bail. Some shut down inside and kept it to themselves, while others dropped out of the journey entirely.

The common religious diagnosis for this phenomenon draws on Jesus's parable of the sower. You hear, "Well, it's sad, but his heart must be rocky soil" or "His spiritual life became choked by weeds."

Maybe, but I wasn't so sure.

The men I knew had real stuff going on in their lives— pain, old wounds, deep complications that left them confused and defeated. Sometimes their unhappiness felt more existential and tougher to pin down. But one thing they knew: another Bible verse or session of prayer wasn't going to fix it.

In YPO, I saw a parallel dynamic. Highly motivated guys—men of various faiths or no faith—would join, get involved, and work hard on building authentic relationships. Then they, too, would hit a wall and eventually drift to the sidelines.

Why? I didn't have the language then for describing what was happening. But now I do, and you do too. The men who hit the wall were being overtaken by an unseen stranger—their own mysterious and powerful subconscious reality. *Their shadow self.*

By the mid-90s, I found myself forum chairman for the Florida YPO chapter and saw an opportunity. I grabbed the chance to start a different kind of forum. Working with a small group of newbies, we designed a forum I'll describe in what follows. Our plan was bold. It drew on what I was learning about why good men end up in trouble. And it ratcheted up the requirements while aiming for nothing less than transformation.

> The men who hit the wall were being overtaken by an unseen stranger—their *shadow self.*

Were we crazy or on to something big? We really didn't know. We just decided that if we weren't in danger of failing at what we were reaching for, we weren't reaching high enough.

The year was 1995.

Twenty-six years later, my original forum is still together. Lives, careers, and marriages have been changed for the better, mine included. We launched another forum for Christian leaders that is now ten years old and has been just as powerful.

I started as leader and teacher. But over time, the other members have all become my teachers—and I couldn't be more grateful.

what happens in a circle

A forum is a safe, confidential environment where men can grow in self-awareness, healing, and spirituality. And growth is about more than getting better or improving our win-loss count.

Ultimately, it's about transformation.

When someone asks me to say *exactly* what happens at forum, I'm still likely to be vague. I tend not to describe in detail what happens for the simple reason that each meeting and group defines its own experience—and is also highly dynamic. We always want to be able to respond in the moment to the energy in the room—to respond to the question, *What is needed now, here, with us?*

My understanding of the potential for honest sharing in small groups has been informed by my "sixty meetings in sixty days" experience in the rooms of AA and Al-Anon. Sitting day after day with hurting people, I saw what happens when people gather with only one item on the agenda: to stay clean and sober today and to do that in the company of others who desperately desire the same thing.

These fearless men and women taught me that *it is the people in the room who bring the healing.* To sit in a circle bound by caring people who give you uninterrupted listening and nonjudgment, to hear others say their honest truth out loud, and to hear yourself saying yours back—that *is* the medicine they come to receive.

> These fearless men and women taught me that *it is the people in the room who bring the healing.*

Jim, an entrepreneur and professional who has held a prominent elected office, describes the impact of shared stories on him. "I discovered that to be invited into other men's stories—the real one, not the image presented to the world at large—is a privilege. Every time. But it also changes me. Each time I have witnessed another man be fiercely authentic and vulnerable, I'm reminded that 'one man's work is every man's work.'"

My thinking on the incredible power of experiential men's groups has also been influenced by, among many others, Shirzad Chamine, CEO emeritus of the Coaches Training Institute and a longtime Stanford faculty member.

Men do not need another program or event, notes Chamine. What they need is an *experience*—one that occurs "deep in the heart, rather than through cool and safe level-headed discussions."[40]

> Men do not need another program or event. What they need is an *experience* that occurs "deep in the heart." -*Shirzad Chamine*

Genuinely transformative groups, he writes, "change the old concepts of what it is to trust another human being, the central role of feelings and emotions, the true priorities of life, the gift of vulnerability, the obsession to be in control, the fear of failure or death, the role of money or power, the beauty of conflict, the self-sabotaging obstacles to intimacy, the search for meaning, the purpose of one's life, and what really constitutes success."[41]

It's fair to say that every big idea on Chamine's inspiring agenda comes up in forums and retreats. They are reflected in our ALL IN value propositions. They explain why we prioritize going deep over programming, knowledge acquisition, or social networking—why our goals tend to be experiential, visual, and relational rather than content based or talk-therapy based.

These are our guiding values:

+ Achieve a greater sense of freedom.
+ Connect to your personal power and creativity.
+ Clarify your life purpose and mission.
+ Experience breakthroughs in areas where you may be stuck.
+ Understand the blind spots that might be holding you back.
+ Create more fulfilling relationships.
+ Explore your spiritual journey.

We show up expecting to take necessary risks.

As you'd expect, an important distinction of ALL IN forums and retreats is our incorporation of shadow work. We draw on the rich insights of Carl Jung and Robert Bly—along with other wisdom, spiritual, and therapeutic traditions—to help men access and heal their inner beings.

Our times together provide forum brothers with the safety and support they need to bring more and more of their hidden selves into the light. Not surprisingly, what begins with emotions often reaches into the spiritual.

Troy, a business owner, told his forum mates that he had grown up essentially as an orphan. Even after he married into a wonderful family, he still felt emotionally alone.

"My forum brothers gave me a platform to delve into my shadow," he said. "In my soul, I did not really believe

178 • all in

God loved me. Through their support I've been able to make significant progress in this darkest area of my life. To connect with God in a way that seemed untenable a few years ago. Many of the men I know have given up, sometimes and very sadly, on life itself.

> Gradually, or even suddenly, the burden lifts. We feel less alone. And we discover that all those painful truths can become gifts.

"It's embarrassing to be that fully exposed, but for me, the reward at the other end was receiving the unmistakable presence of God revealed to me in the consistent and unwavering support of my brothers."

The surprise that Troy and others discover is that in the middle of a loyal, like-minded community of men, a miracle occurs. Instead of feeling more shame, we are relieved of it. Instead of confirming that we are uniquely awful, we discover we are perfectly human.

Gradually, or even suddenly, the burden lifts. We feel less alone. And we discover that all those painful truths about our lives that we hoped to keep buried can become gifts that help us create strong, redemptive relationships.

Something else happens too.

We discover that when we take risks to be vulnerable, we invite others to do the same. By witnessing another man's healing journey, we find strength to begin our own.

Often it's a journey of minutes, not months, because once our wounds, confusions, and sad stories are out in the open, we discover that we can *work with them* and not be *controlled by them*. We can see more clearly a path to resolving conflicts and making positive changes in our lives.

In the company of other men, we begin to mend our broken lives and find a new way of being in the world.

three stages of forums

In recent years, YPO International and other leadership, business, church, and personal groups have embraced the value of this type of deeper, more intimate, and more personal forum experience.[42] This kind of forum truly changes lives, as it has ours. The new name for this is, appropriately, transformational forum.

What makes it so different?

Shirzad Chamine describes the three forum stages. In a healthy environment, forums can evolve from social, to substantive, to transformational:

Social forums. This is the common approach of professional or personal groups that focus on fun and gather around common interests. The level of personal disclosure, trust, or intimacy that the members experience is not very different from what they might have experienced either in other cohesive social groups or in other professional groups such as a good board of advisers. Often worthwhile but not special.

Substantive forums. Substantive groups still operate on a paradigm of "more and better" but begin to feel special and unique. You're more likely to experience a higher level of trust, more caring, better discussions, and better results than you will in other relationships.

Many members say the group is the most caring, trusting, and helpful group they have ever belonged to.

So why mess with that?

Because, as Chamine explains, "the underlying belief systems, mental frameworks and paradigms about oneself, life, and work remain fairly intact."

Transformational forums. These groups, according to Chamine,

> challenge some of the fundamental mental and emotional frameworks and paradigms of members in ways that forever change them. They reorder old concepts of what it is to trust another human being, the central role of feelings and emotions, the true priorities of life, the gift of vulnerability, the obsession to be in control, the fear of failure or death, the role of money or power, the beauty of conflict, the self-sabotaging obstacles to intimacy, the search for meaning, the purpose of one's life, and what really constitutes success. These shifts occur deep in the heart, deep in one's bones, as a result of powerful, goosebumps, emotionally riveting experiences with fellow members.

This is what we experience in our ALL IN transformational retreats and monthly forums.

Transformational forums exhibit the following characteristics, writes Chamine:

- Members describe their forum experience as life-changing.

* Every member feels unconditionally loved and respected by all others for exactly who they are.
* Members don't hold anything back in fear of losing respect, love, or influence in the forum.
* Members are willing to be vulnerable and admit to shortcomings. "Looking good" is not a high value.
* Members tell one another the hard truths out of commitment to one another's growth.
* There is no sideline gossip between any members about any others.
* Occasional conflict is recognized, aired fully, and worked through. Members do not pretend conflict doesn't exist.
* There are no outlying members or black sheep. All members are equally "in."
* Without a hierarchy or power structure, it is truly a forum of peers.
* Forum meetings are often deeply moving, not just practical and helpful.

There are no outlying members or black sheep. All members are equally "in."

If you're like me, even a cursory glance at this list of attributes will convince you that a group experience of this sort is exactly what you have long looked for and perhaps thought didn't exist. Fortunately, it can and does! I can't imagine going through the trials and challenges of life without the strength and brotherhood of a transformational forum.

If you are interested, ALL IN can help you create this kind of forum or retreat experience.

safeguarding the miracle

For the rest of this chapter, I want to talk about how we protect the quality of the experience at ALL IN forums and retreats. I don't share this to convince you that ours is the only way, but to help you see what works for us and why and to suggest a group experience you might want to support.

Think of the following group practices as bumpers at a speedway or safety gear on a motorcycle. They're not what gives you the thrill, but they definitely protect you while you're riding high—and you're much more likely to come back for more.

safeguard #1: confidentiality

We regularly affirm our mutual guarantee of confidentiality. We describe it as a pledge to share "Nothing to Nobody, Never."

It's that simple—and hard. I've found you have to *learn* how to guard privacy to this degree because it just doesn't come naturally. But once learned, the practice returns enormous value in all of your relationships.

Some of us may have hoped to find confidential relationships in our church or synagogue. But, for whatever the reason, those spaces can rarely deliver. They return other important benefits, but guarding privacy is rarely one of them.

I remember when a man new to the forum experience stood up and announced, "I don't believe your pledge of confidentiality. I know for a fact there is no such thing!"

He was the senior pastor of a large church.

"Every time I have entrusted someone with a personal problem in confidence, I have been betrayed," he said. "Not once, but again and again and again. In fact, no one has ever *not* betrayed my confidentiality! As a minister, I sometimes feels like anything I say can and will be used against me in the court of public opinion."

I'm sure you can relate. The further up the ladder we go, the more common and devastating the betrayals become. At the top tiers of business, church, and entertainment, our odds of finding safety and privacy on confidential matters are approximately zilch.

> **We describe it as a pledge to share nothing to nobody, never.**

That's why at ALL IN, we take a strictly all or nothing approach to maintaining confidences. That might mean, for example, behaving as if you hardly know a man whose name comes up in conversation, even though he may be one of your closest forum mates.

safeguard #2: clear intention

Why would busy leaders be willing to invest so much time in an uncomfortable, sometimes demanding group encounter?

The answer is simple. They hate mediocrity. They have learned that committed relationships take time. And they come to a group with a clear intention to realize *more of what they could be* and *less of what they have been.*

184 • all in

In other words, they are willing to go all in.

Forging real connections between men require us to slow down, feel, and listen to ourselves when our natural tendency may be to speed up and stay busy.

What kind of companion do you want alongside when you are trying to own up to the parts of your life that take every ounce of courage just to say out loud? I know I want a man who hates to settle and doesn't want me to either. A fellow striver who's just as motivated as I am to reach for more.

> **Forging real connections between men require us to slow down, feel, and listen to ourselves.**

In his book *The Way of the Superior Man*, David Deida writes,

Your close men friends should be willing to challenge your mediocrity by suggesting a concrete action you can perform that will pop you out of your rut, one way or the other. And you must be willing to offer them your brutal honesty, in the same way, if you are all to grow.[43]

Deida doesn't mean "superior" in the sense of hierarchy or acclaim. For him, the word describes the highest and best to which a man can aspire.

Look around the circle at a transformational forum and you will find men who aspire to this kind of greatness. They are brought together by a powerful intention to live wholeheartedly. Their cultural and religious backgrounds will definitely influence how they describe that intention for themselves. But I guarantee it will have nothing to do with the usual trappings of ego or worldly success.

In my experience, every good candidate for healing feels driven by a clear intention to be a better, more authentic man.

safeguard #3: commitment

We "take in" a ball game. We might "attend" church. But for a forum or retreat to become transformational, members need to be personally invested. As we often say, you have to "fully show up" for the miracle.

> We "take in" a ball game....But for a forum or retreat to become transformational, members need to be personally invested.

Men who are only "fairly committed" tend to shut down when things get uncomfortable or hide behind pseudo-intimacy. And personal change or growth just can't occur.

That's why we start a new forum by asking for certain commitments:

- You agree to attend all scheduled monthly meetings and two retreats. No exceptions.
- You agree to commit for one year.
- You agree to start every meeting or event on time.

If these requirements sound unreasonable, I'd understand. Extenuating circumstances do occur, and we deal with those with grace.

And creativity. Once when I was late, I was asked to sit in the middle of the circle while each man shared the sacrifices he had made to get there on time, and how it felt to him when I made everyone wait. That did *not* feel good, but I came away with a new perspective.

Our conditions for membership are high because our expectations for the experience we create together are high. We've found that making sacrifices to honor other members brings enormous meaning, especially when things in our personal lives get tough.

Jeff, to whom I introduced you in chapter 6, knows firsthand what that looks like. He went through the excruciating experience of losing his wife to cancer when she was only forty-one. She and Jeff battled the disease together for more than two years. Throughout that time, his forum stood by him and his family.

One of his wife's treatment cycles required her to spend two months in Chicago undergoing intensive treatment. "I was with her every step of the way and, many times, spent the night in her hospital room on the little bench seat. It was a time I desperately needed my forum's support but could not get home for the monthly meeting. My forum all changed plans and came to Chicago for the meeting! It was an incredible display of love and support, one that my wife and I both deeply appreciated."

Sometime later, while Jeff was attending a forum meeting, he got the call he dreaded. His wife had taken a sharp turn for the worse.

"My entire forum went with me to the hospital!" Jeff recalls. One mate took charge of arranging hospice care. Two others spent the night with him. When she passed the next day, forum mates took care of the funeral arrangements with the funeral home, helped craft an obituary, and took photographs and video of the memorial service.

In the days and weeks following, they brought food to the house and took his boys bowling. "It was the most difficult time of my life. But they kept picking me up and dusting me off every step of the way, until I could get back on my feet."

safeguard #4: clearing

Think about the number of times someone in a small group you were part of got offended or annoyed, began to distance themselves from others, and then maybe dropped out. Maybe that person was you.

I don't believe it is possible to go through this life without bumping into other people in hurtful ways. The more engaged we are with the world, the more relationships we have, the more this is likely to happen. It only makes sense, then, that every major spiritual tradition teaches that keeping short accounts, asking for forgiveness often, and making amends however we can are at the heart of maturity.

Whenever we throw all our energies and resources toward achieving something important, we create friction. We *will* brush up against others in a way that can leave them feeling bruised. Without a way to address and resolve tensions, disagreements, and conflicts when they arise, a group is likely to devolve into a disappointing experience for everyone.

The safeguard of clearing (sometimes called "cleansing the container") is a healing protocol or series of steps we follow that shows men how to confront and resolve relationship issues we'd rather avoid.

On its surface, clearing may not seem like such a big deal to you. But in my twenty-six years of participating in transformational forums and retreats, I have found this safeguard to be the single most powerful tool for change. And not just in the group. It models how to work through conflicts in every relationship, whether that is our marriage, with our children, at work, or with friends.

> In my twenty-six years, I have found this safeguard to be the single most powerful tool for change.

What we pick up as kids rarely helps us resolve conflict in healthy ways. My natural response from my childhood was to respond to criticism or confrontation by quickly and profusely apologizing. Why? For a people pleaser like me (see chapter 4), criticism feels like a punch in the nose. I learned that apologizing quickly helped me escape further embarrassment.

I simply thought, *If I apologize, maybe they will shut up.*

Compare that coping strategy to patiently hearing out another man's anger toward you without interruption, judgment, or self-defense. That takes guts, yet I've found it is the most profound way to honor others and fully hear for ourselves what we need in order to grow. In fact, I have come to believe that the greatest gift we can give a person we have injured is *not* an apology—at least not at first—but an openness to receive all of what they have to say, then demonstrate to the person that they have been fully heard.

In forums, we break clearing into steps. We call it "Quarter Talk" because there are four essential parts, sometimes a fifth (if you're a therapist or spiritual director, these steps may be familiar to you):

> I have come to believe that the greatest gift we can give a person we have injured is *not* an apology.

- **Facts.** I state the facts about the incident as I see them and without interruption.
- **Feelings.** I put words to all the feelings I am aware that I have about the incident.
- **Judgments.** My judgments lead me to the feelings about the other person and the incident.
- **Wants.** The experience requires me to decide: What is it that I want? To be heard? To see a change in the other person's behavior? To fix what is broken? The practice of clearing makes it safe to share that.

The fifth and more advanced step is this:
- **My part.** I own what part I had in the originating experience—what I could have said or done differently and how I contributed in some way to my own injury.

I've learned that there may be nothing as healing and satisfying as hearing my own words spoken back to me and knowing that, without interruption or excuses or defensiveness, I have been heard.

Some call it the *awesome power of the listening ear.*

We have often started a retreat or a forum meeting with a full agenda, then found ourselves spending the next four to six hours in courageous sharing and listening. It is never time misspent. We come away with a powerful sense of cleansing and an experience of honesty, safety, and intimacy in relationships that few men will ever know.

higher up and further in—the power of time away

Something powerful happens to men when they get away from their comfortable routine environment on a three- to four-day ALL IN retreat with a skilled facilitator in a confidential, safe environment.

We call these times away "superchargers" because of the effect they have on participants. What follows here can give you only a glimpse into their power.

An ALL IN retreat is not for drinking, golfing, fishing, gambling, or entertainment. There may be a recreational component, and it may be intense, competitive, and playful, but we come together in a thoughtfully curated adventure with our focus on relationship building and inner work.

This can be especially true when participants who come to a retreat are also committed to a transformational forum. The safeguards are understood and applied, and we meet with a shared clear intention to use the time to push to our individual edge.

Whether we go to an exotic locale or somewhere familiar, the key elements of a transformative retreat always include the following:

Unhurried time. To slow down, listen to your own heart, calm your mind, and escape from the constant distractions of your ringing telephone, chirping text messages, distracting emails, and daily responsibilities.

At our first retreat, facilitator Jim Warner had us plot our life story on a single graph, showing the life experiences in high points and low points. We filled in not just the events but also our reactions to them and why. For example, we included why we were excited, happy, or affirmed or why we were depressed, angry, sad, lonely, or scared. The exercise took hours, but it was a revelation to see our life stories charted on a single graph.

> The safeguards are understood and applied, and we meet with a shared clear intention to use the time to push to our individual edge.

Experiential processing. Becoming aware of any anger, fear, sadness, grief, and anxiety you may be carrying. To do this, we create safe opportunities for each man to patiently and voluntarily explore difficult feelings, such as fear. Whether we are hiking the desert mountains of Mexico or whitewater rafting in Montana, activities are designed to push men to their edges.

Music. Music and scents are sometimes able to connect us with our emotions and memories more powerfully than conscious thought.

Solitude and intentional play. These are powerful elements that can help us move our bodies, break loose things we cannot see and release, and adequately consider during our normal routine of life or even during a short forum meeting.

Connection with nature. Immersion in wild places—whether in the mountains or desert, forests or ocean—helps evoke in us a nearly magical healing force.

the wholehearted life

I remember a man I'll call Greg, who said at one of our retreats that he had never been able to be honest with anyone about his secret life, hardly even with himself. And he happened to lead a large ministry that had touched thousands. That made his struggle all the lonelier and more excruciating.

In a letter to me after the event, he described his condition on arrival: "On a scale of one to ten, with one being suicidal and ten being euphoric, I was a two and had been that way for several weeks. But God used that group of men and our facilitator to give me a breakthrough in my depression and my sexual addiction."

He sees now that the breakthroughs could never have happened without a group of men committed to honesty and absolute confidentiality there and later. "I thank God that even though my sins are many, His grace is more. He has used my struggles for His glory and my good," he wrote. "I am grateful from the bottom of my heart."

I love stories like Greg's. You can feel the relief radiating from every word. You can sense new hope springing up.

Social scientist and author Brené Brown captures the miracle of the circle when she says, "I believe that vulnerability—the willingness to show up and be seen with no guarantee of outcome—is the only path to more love, belonging, and joy. Even in the midst of struggle, I would say that doing this work is not only worth it; it is *the work* of living a wholehearted life."[44]

> I love stories like Greg's. You can feel the relief radiating from every word.

That hits home for me.

I can truly say that these men in my forums are my closest and dearest friends in the world. They know the good and bad about me and all my idiosyncrasies. They help me to see my blind spots—my shadow. They can tell me when they see I am full of crap or simply wrong, then offer forgiveness, reconciliation, and a hug. That's Samwise and Frodo in *The Lord of the Rings*, but for real.

That's a fellowship of imperfect, superior men.

pause to reflect

1. The heart of this chapter is the principle that men are best able to change and thrive when we're part of a certain kind of group. In your own words, how would you describe that group?

2. Why do you think men struggle so much to be forthcoming about our secret struggles?

3. What risks are you willing to take to reach for personal growth and change in a "pack"?

For more free resources, see

CHAPTER 10

everything that matters

What does it profit a man to gain the whole world, yet forfeit his soul?

—Jesus of Nazareth

THE GOAL OF THIS BOOK HAS BEEN TO MOTIVATE YOU to do the hard work of uncovering your true self: of looking deep inside for clues to what drives us—and sometimes drives us wrong.

This hard work comes with great risk and even greater promise.

But the very fact that you're reading this page tells me you will sign up for difficult, scary, interior work—and stick with it—*if that's what it takes to grow, heal, and change.*

It's like we have hiked the Appalachian Trail together, and we have arrived at Mount Mitchell (elevation 6,684 feet), the highest point between Georgia and Maine. Miles and miles of the Great Smokies roll away from us on all sides. The view is breathtaking!

Now it's time to look ahead.

And time for me to ask, *What will you do with all this?*

Will you just say, "That's interesting," but keep living the way you always have? Or are you ready to get unstuck? Go *all in?*

The fact is this—a life is possible now that wasn't before. That's because a man who commits to hard inner work is empowered for change. He is equipped to know himself and others more authentically. He feels more integrated in his beliefs, thoughts, and emotions. He can now live more intentionally and enjoy relationships that really work.

He is on what Deida dares to call "the way of the superior man"[45]—that is, a man who chooses to evolve, who is reaching for both strength and heart.

This is my story, and I hope it is becoming yours.

In this chapter, we bring it all together by tackling three enormous but very practical applications—each one a hard-earned prize:

> The fact is this—a life is possible now that wasn't before.

+ How we can find our passion.
+ How we can know and embrace our purpose.
+ How our passion and purpose can lead us into a new, larger life.

Hold tight! Your best future is straight ahead.

bricks and bare feet: a rediscovery of passion

My own awakening began after I had run myself and my most important relationships into the ditch. I had no choice but to reach for help.

One day, when I was still getting the hang of "feeling what I was feeling," the coach I hired to guide me decided I was ready for more advanced stuff. I needed to work on "the body-mind connection," he said.

His solution was martial arts training.

Reconnecting body and mind made sense, I thought. Sort of. After all, what landed me on the injured list at work and at home was a growing *dis*connection. I had lost touch with the inner fire that drove me around the racetrack day after day. I had found myself galloping at full speed without knowing why anymore. I had let my most important relationships languish.

But still. Martial arts?

Had Racehorse Allen's brilliant career come down to "wax on, wax off" with Mr. Miyagi?

I never considered myself an athlete. In high school, my greatest athletic achievement was being the school photographer who chronicled the achievements of others.

Yet trading in my starched white shirt and cuff links for a simple white karate uniform brought me a sense of fun and freedom. Right from the start in the dojang (a Tae Kwon Do studio), I noticed that I felt like a six-year-old child again.

> I had lost touch with the inner fire that drove me around the racetrack day after day.

The bare feet helped. So did the fact that, in class, we were all anonymous. That meant I had no one to impress, no one with whom to exchange business cards. That safe, affirming atmosphere energized me to try new things.

My sensei, Grand Master Diego Perez, taught me the disciplines of breath and posture, of showing respect and honor to the "enemy," and of mastering the ancient skills to attack and defend using only the body.

Soon I wondered if it would be possible to advance through the ten belt levels to become a black belt by the time I turned fifty. (You can see that my type A, achievement-oriented personality had come on sabbatical with me!)

But that birthday was just sixteen months away. Was my goal even possible?

My sensei sounded encouraging but set high expectations. He said I would need to train one to two hours a day for six days a week.

I threw myself into my new "business." Slowly I built strength, breaking through one mental barrier after another.

As I proceeded through nine belt levels and approached my physical fitness training requirements for my first-degree black belt test, I realized I had to demonstrate that I could do one hundred push-ups in under two minutes. As hard as I could push myself, I could do only sixty push-ups. Clearly, an explanation was in order.

I announced to my teacher for this stage, Master Mary Beth Perez, that my body would do only sixty. I was not like the teenagers in the dojang, after all. (With two Perez sensei to one Morris in the dojang, I figured I really needed to stand up for myself!)

She said, "Great. Let me see your sixty push-ups."

I gave it all I had and collapsed after sixty, proving to her that was all I could do. She affirmed me on my accomplishment and told me to take a rest.

After some conversation, she said, "Okay. Let's push out twenty more together."

Apprehensively, I agreed to try. I did so, shaky and exhausted, and collapsed again.

More rest and casual conversation.

"Now, let's push out twenty more together." By then, I could see what she was doing.

Massive effort, another collapse. More rest and conversation.

"And now another ten."

Which—somehow—I did.

"See," Sensei Perez announced. "You did one hundred push-ups. You know you can do it. Now all you have to do is shorten the time."

What had just happened? *She had proven to me that I could do what I knew for a fact, and with certainty, I could not do!*

> She had proven to me that I could do what I knew for a fact, and with certainty, I could not do!

The next month when I tested for my first-degree black belt, I peeled off one hundred push-ups in one minute and sixteen seconds.

less effort, more power

One day in the dojang, as I was learning a new sequence of moves, Grand Master Diego Perez said, "Mr. Morris, you are not pleased with your progress?"

"What do you mean?" I asked.

He replied, "You are making a face that you are not happy."

"I am?"

I was not even aware that my face showed the strain or that I was angry with myself for not doing my kicks as well as I wanted.

Grand Master Perez proposed an experiment. He set up a punching bag with sensors to measure the pounds per square inch of impact in my kick. Then he invited me to apply my best form to deliver my most powerful kicks to the bag.

Front kick. Round kick. Sidekick... I really let 'er have it!

Grand Master Perez's calm exterior betrayed no hint of how he judged my performance. Apparently, I had not impressed him.

But he had new instructions. "Now relax. Have fun. Be playful and feel your joy. *Then* kick the bag."

Relax? Play? It was my turn to be unimpressed.

Yes, Sensei, I thought. *I'll do that. But why are we messing around here?* Nevertheless...

I laughed. I bounced. I played. I joked. Then...

Front kick. Round kick. Sidekick. And I let the bag have it again!

I'll never forget that experience. The sensors showed I had delivered 50 percent more power to the bag! My kick had become powerful enough, said Grand Master Perez, to break a man's femur—the largest bone in the body.

"Relax. Have fun. Be playful and feel your joy. *Then* kick the bag."

I was dumbfounded. It had never crossed my mind that relaxing into the sheer pleasure of the sport might release more power than ratcheting up the pressure to perform.

And that's when it dawned on me: it's not in the quest for perfection. The power is in the passion. *My power is greatest when I am directly connected to my passion.*

With a renewed sense of possibilities, I followed Grand Master Perez's instructions further until I was performing feats in the dojang that had always seemed out of reach.

I broke through a block of wood with one chop. In time, I broke through four.

One day, I discovered another "impossibility." While holding a block with one hand and no one holding the other end, I could chop the block into a crazy explosion of bits!

What self-limiting belief did I have in other areas of my life?

Martial arts training was revealing its wisdom to me. In a nutshell, I was learning that, with all my education, *I had no idea what I was capable of doing when my body and mind were in alignment.*

What self-limiting belief did I have in other areas of my life?

I had somehow never internalized the fact that trying harder and working longer hours is no substitute for passion and can never by itself get us where we most want to go.

My intended brief experience at forty-eight years old turned out to be such a revelation that I continued the training to become a black belt. But once I achieved that goal, I kept on going.

Second-degree black belt. Third degree. Fourth degree.

Twelve years and four black belts later, I became a Tae Kwon Do Master … because I was *having fun and connected to my passion.*

fire and wind

In a business or professional context, we think of passion as the level of commitment and enthusiasm team members bring through the door every day. Or to put it in figures of speech: passion is the fire in your bones. It's—to rip off the pop song—the wind beneath your wings.

Passion helps us reach our full potential while enjoying the ride.

Of course, we've all seen what apathy looks like. It's not pretty. We can have coworkers who are tremendously capable, but if they're not all in, or if what they do isn't tapping into their joy at some level, they're just adding deadweight to the operation.

> When we talk about passion, we mean *a powerful, joyful drive at the core of a man's being.*

At ALL IN, when we talk about passion, we mean *a powerful, joyful drive at the core of a man's being* that gives him a special sense of calling and the intense desire to pursue it with gusto.

Whenever we bring passion to a task, we find ourselves naturally doing it with zeal and excellence. When I'm flying a plane, racing a motorcycle, or taking my grandkids out on the boat to catch fish, I bring my very best—and time flies by unnoticed.

What does passion look like on your weekend?

I have one of Joseph Campbell's quotes carved into a stone bench near our log cabin in the mountains of North Carolina. The bench is on a path my wife, June, and I call our "Wisdom

Walk," and I've noticed that visitors from men's and women's groups who use the cabin feel drawn to the spot.

The quote reads, "Follow your bliss and the universe will open doors where there were only walls."

That, to me, is the power of passion!

But what about those times when bliss has left the building? When we can't find that open door Campbell talks about?

I learned that a simple question can come to the rescue.

> "What do you want?" Just those four words. It may be the most mysterious question in the universe.

what do you want?

One of the easiest questions to ask, yet hardest to answer, is "What do you want?" Just those four words. It may be the most mysterious question in the universe.

If you have trouble knowing what you feel genuinely passionate about, I recommend you sit with the question on a regular basis and ask it in the following ways.

What *do* I want?

What do *I* want?

What do I *want*?

In the profound comedy *Bruce Almighty*, the TV news anchor Bruce Nolan (played by Jim Carrey) rages at God (Morgan Freeman) about unanswered prayers. So when God hands divine power over to him, Nolan decides every request will get a "Yes!" from heaven—only to have chaos ensue.

He whines to God, "Why are they so unhappy? I gave them what they wanted!"

To which God replies, "Since when do people know what they want?"

Hmm.

Do I really know what I want? Do you?[46]

I'd have to say most people I meet don't. For long stretches in my life, I didn't either. And I find that I must regularly circle around to ask the question again— because the answer keeps changing.

But this is where shadow work can help.

My friend Barry, a company president at the time, often shared his struggle with chronic unhappiness in our twenty-six-year forum

> "A part of me did not want to know what I wanted, because *if I did know, I would have to do something about it.*"

we were a part of. Each month he would share that he was still trying to get to the bottom of it. For him, a turning point came when a forum mate looked him in the eye and asked, "Do you really *want* to know what you want?"

"In that moment," Barry recalls, "my soul was deeply moved. I realized that a part of me did not want to know what I wanted, because *if I did know, I would have to do something about it.*"

Subconsciously, he had been keeping himself disconnected from his passion to protect himself from the risk of taking action.

Like Barry, I couldn't see what I had been missing until another person showed me. One day in a conversation with my coach that had wandered to the topic of airplanes, he made an unusual observation.

"You know, Allen, when you talk about flying, your whole face changes. Your eyes brighten up, even your skin tone changes. I think you should explore flying again."

Those words hit me like the screech of a metal detector at the beach as it passes over a gold doubloon! He had detected bliss. In me!

I had been too close to see it in myself, but he could.

He had detected bliss. In me!

In chapter 5, I told you that I'd been hooked on flying from the time I first got my pilot's license in the Georgia Tech flying club. But over the years, the demands of business, marriage, and children had accomplished what that crash on I-20 couldn't—they pushed the joy of flying right out of my life.

And I had let it stay out.

But now my coach had reconnected me with the incredible rush I felt when I was soaring through the skies. I decided to take his question as "permission" to fly again.

I reactivated my pilot's license and started my training. On my first fully recertified solo flight, when I climbed out alone, I let out a scream of joy so loud I think they heard me five thousand feet below!

That was the sound of my bliss.

Reconnecting with our unique passion can drive us to new heights. For me that was reached again later, flying five hundred miles per hour at forty-five thousand feet of altitude as an FAA-certified jet pilot.

purpose: how passion becomes direction

A man's quest for passion strikes me as closely related to our visceral need for purpose. In fact, I have come to believe that passion and purpose are inextricably linked, and together they want to lead us to great things.

Every man I know struggles at times to identify why he's on earth. *What am I working so hard for, anyway? What difference do I make?* Sooner or later, our hypercompetitive natures need to take more home than just another win.

> **What am I working so hard for, anyway? What difference do I make?**

We need meaning. We want significance.

If our passion is the unique, joyful desire that drives us, then purpose is what gives our passion direction.

The day I walked out of the office on my sabbatical, I knew I had lost both. I felt emotionally disconnected from what used to consume me.

But I was changing. Finding new mind-body connections with Grand Master Perez and screaming with joy in the cockpit of my Piper had given me a taste of happiness. And I wanted more.

After all, a man's purpose must be about more than portfolios and ROIs. More than about me, too, for that matter.

Campbell described what purpose means for men on a quest. He wrote, "A hero is someone who has given his or her life to something bigger than oneself."

Another word for that is *mission*.

> "A hero is someone who has given his or her life to something bigger than oneself." -Joseph Campbell

My interior journey had made me aware that repressed and misdirected parts of me had been draining my spiritual tank. The more connected I felt to my healthy self, the closer I got to a sense of purpose. And the more its scope grew.

Every businessman knows that companies try to capture their most important corporate purpose in a mission statement. Our company mission statement was formal and proper, and I intellectually agreed with it. But I realized what we had was not really an expression of my passion or joy.

As I mulled this over with our leadership team, we discovered that none of us could recite our existing formal mission statement. We all agreed that our new one should be simple, clear, and highly motivating.

It was time for a rewrite.

Long days of discussing, reflecting, and scribbling out possibilities followed. I desperately wanted a statement that harnessed our passion and purpose for great things.

This time, when I asked myself, *What do I want?* I found that I wanted to capture that "something bigger" quality Campbell wrote about. I realized that what I wanted now was leading me to ask, *How can I help?*

As a real estate developer who had set out on a hero's journey, I wanted a sense of purpose that went beyond buildings and property. "Something bigger" for me had to be about people. And it had to make room for bliss.

What I wanted now was to bless and inspire others, as so many have blessed and inspired me; to surprise people with more than they expected; and to make peoples' lives better.

These statements, we decided, took us almost all the way home. For our real estate development and service business, the mission ultimately distilled down to this:

- *Inspire people with the beauty of our projects.*
- *Impress them with the excellence of their experience.*
- *Improve the lives of everyone we touch.*

Inspire. Impress. Improve.

There it was—in three sentences and in three words.

when business and personal converge

When our mission first went up on the flip chart and I said it out loud, tears welled up. Chills ran through my body. Something about this had touched a deep part of my soul. I couldn't quite put my finger on it, but it felt to me like joy combined with a reason to come thundering out of the starting gate every morning.

We took our new vision and framed it for the walls, printed it in our brochures, featured it on websites, and emblazoned it on our coffee mugs.

Seeing our purpose in writing brought immediate tangible rewards. First, as a team, we had a measuring stick for evaluating what we would do and not do as a company. If a project ignited our passion and fulfilled our purpose, we could confidently and enthusiastically embrace it. If not, we moved on.

Second, our new mission brought clarity to me as the leader—and clarity is a critical quality for any leader.

> Turning passion into purpose...leads us to our true vocation in life.

In the years since, "Inspire, Impress, Improve" has led us to create one award-winning project after another, and the business is continuing to evolve as we respond to the changing economy and culture.

For example, I had thought of myself as an office building developer specializing in 50,000 to 150,000-square-foot office buildings. Honestly, I had been stuck in that limiting belief for a very long time. But I realized my boundaries had been entirely self-imposed. When my visionary son suggested we develop large condominiums and apartment buildings, we did our homework, then launched a new company to do just that.

To be honest, it wasn't until much later, as I was preparing my annual life plan, that I fully understood why those three words had brought me to tears when I read it out loud in front of my team.

I saw that the company mission connected so deeply with me *because it was also my life mission!* How could something so obvious have been so overlooked by me?

In my life I want to inspire others with a vision of great possibilities. I want to impress others with God's healing love. And I want to improve the lives of those around me.

Empowered by this larger purpose that integrated and focused all my energies, I understood what C. S. Lewis meant when he wrote, "A sense of divine vision must be restored to man's daily work."[47]

The vision continues to shape my life. Instead of developing office buildings that are just pretty and profitable, I now only care to design and develop projects that truly infuse people and communities with joy, meaning, and significance.

> We all deserve to spend our time and energy in a direction that makes us smile, gives us chills, and, every now and then, brings tears of joy to our eyes!

Turning passion into purpose—whether in business or in our personal lives—is a lifelong and difficult journey. But it leads us to our true vocation in life—the place where, as Frederick Buechner says, "your deep gladness and the world's deep hunger meet."[48]

My stumbling journey in that direction has taught me I can reach peak performance—and sustain it—only when my work mission and life mission converge.

We all deserve to spend our time and energy in a direction that makes us smile, gives us chills, and, every now and then, brings tears of joy to our eyes!

And we can.

from rude awakening to joy

The first few years I knew a CEO named John, I experienced him as a guarded, angry man. That scared me because anger was part of my own childhood wound. But to find healing, he was committed to "peeling the onion" in forums and retreats.

Now as he looks back, he sees three important shifts that connected him with his passion and purpose.

The first came at a retreat after he had a very rude awakening.

"I realized that I was out of integrity," he told me. "To put it plainly, that I did not speak my truth. I lied and manipulated people."

John says he had to learn how to step out of pride and into humility. That changed so much for him. "I learned to lower my guard and step into intimacy in my relationships, especially with Deb [his wife] but also with the forum."

"A core question at a retreat was, 'Do you wake up every day and love what you do?'"

The second shift helped him shed a powerful self-limiting belief that he was not creative.

"The facilitator challenged me on that. Then he helped me fundamentally reframe my assumptions," he said. A new connection to his playful side empowered him to express himself in ways he hadn't before, especially in his photography.

The biggest shift occurred in how he thought about his work.

"A core question at a retreat was, 'Do you wake up every day and love what you do?' I couldn't bring myself to answer that," he said.

With the help of others, John began to implement important changes. One was to develop a deeper sense of curiosity in his life and to look at things in a much deeper way. The second was shifting from serving self to serving others. "That opened my life to fulfillment and joy," he said.

John's transformation has been truly beautiful to observe. And it continues to lead him in new directions. He published two books that feature his art and photography. And he has now left his CEO position to facilitate retreats and coach others in their journeys full-time.

free to dare

Have you witnessed people you care about change right before your eyes? And then pursue new possibilities packed with joy, meaning, and significance?

John's example inspires me. As do the other stories of men in these pages who have dared to know and name their truth—and then do what it takes to change. They remind me to measure my life not by my fear but by the courage it took to get me here. And by outcomes, especially those I never thought could happen before I started the journey.

They prove to me that when we commit to the difficult path toward wholeness, the outcomes make the journey worthwhile.

214 • all in

For example, we discover the freedom to dare greatly in small and large things. We can take the apostle Paul's astounding claim as our own: "It is for freedom that Christ has set us free."[49]

You remember I told you that I used to think of myself as an office building developer who specialized (successfully) in a variety of strictly sensible office buildings? And that I had been stuck in that frame of mind for a very long time?

We discover the freedom to dare greatly in small and large things.

Reconnecting with my passion and purpose really did a number on that belief!

As I began my own journey into the shadow, I sensed a growing courage to dream big, and of daring to bring those dreams to life. One accomplishment early in my journey symbolizes to me the rewards of taking the dare.

I found myself imagining an office building like nothing I'd seen before. The vision was not measured in cost per square foot or by trends I'd seen in the trade publications. It came from the timeless cathedrals of Spain.

I called it Alhambra Towers, a jewel of an office building that I envisioned becoming the defining icon of Coral Gables, the strategic center of Greater Miami.

For a businessman who had worked his way up developing cost-efficient office buildings, I can tell you this line of thinking really scared me!

To realize the dream, we would have to spend far more than any normal office building would call for. We would have to find corporate tenants willing to pay a higher rent than had ever been paid in any office building in Miami, Florida.

And to see it through, I'd have to commit myself heart, soul, and wallet.

It was what I call a roll of the platinum dice.

Some like to say that real estate is all about location, location, location. That sounds clever, but it's baloney.

Let's be real: major office buildings, like other sizable development or business ventures, do not succeed for only one reason, or simply because you sincerely want them to. After more than eighty-five successful development projects, I can tell you that success is *always* the result of a combination of factors. Those include concept, architecture, planning, budgeting, financing, location, execution of details, political support, sensitivity to the local culture, market research, marketing and leasing, property management, capital reserves, and, most importantly, a great team.

> To see it through, I'd have to commit myself heart, soul, and wallet.

Also, location. That's big.

And let's not forget elements beyond our control, such as the good fortune of delivering your new baby into a healthy economy that welcomes you with minimum direct competition.

But when you are powered by passion and purpose, you are perfectly positioned to put your newfound freedom and courage to the test.

Against considerable odds, our dream building went up. And up.

The $100-million-plus Alhambra Towers now stands in the heart of Coral Gables as a remarkable business and civic achievement. The building is anchored by three towers, the tallest of which stands at 295 feet, making it second only to the historic Coral Gables Biltmore Hotel. The west tower is adorned with a twelve-foot-tall working weather vane that is an exact replica of the original "Lady of Faith" weather vane atop the Giralda Tower in Seville, Spain. A carillon in the west tower marks the hour by playing from a repertoire of nearly two thousand hymns, bells, tolls, and classic chimes.

> Inside, imported stone, Etruscan-style alabaster chandeliers from Spain, and rich attention to color and texture bring pleasure at every turn.

Inside, imported stone, Etruscan-style alabaster chandeliers from Spain, and rich attention to color and texture bring pleasure at every turn.

I share these design details for one reason: to illustrate how passion can motivate us to achieve great things, whether it is harnessed in our life's work or, as in John's case, some other creative pursuit.

Alhambra Towers has been featured on the city's website and planning guide, in chamber of commerce materials, and on magazine and book covers. It has been honored as the Commercial Building of the Year in Florida and has since won ten awards.

Today, it is home to our Allen Morris Company corporate headquarters.

Was realizing the dream a cakewalk? No.

In the rough-and-tumble competitive, and sometimes brutal, world of commercial real estate development, we encountered an onslaught of challenges. (I'll spare you the list.) But, week by week, we persevered, and one by one we overcame each challenge.

> What took me so long to figure out that my work should be more than my training, capability, and opportunity?

When our team stepped back and saw what we had created, I thought, *Why didn't we always build buildings like that?*

What took me so long to figure out that my work should be more than my training, capability, and opportunity?

When I walk through the doors these days, I am reminded that my whole life must be about more than an expression of my training, capabilities, and opportunity. It must express what I value most.

And magnificent structures only hint at what that might be.

the rest of the story

The older I get, the more I notice that my life story shows itself in strands. Probably everyone's does. Recreational obsessions (most of them having to do with driving fast cars and also flying fast), business, church and ministry responsibilities, my spiritual path, my marriage and my family. They wind around one another to make up the whole of my life—and my life is blessed, for sure.

But for me, there's one strand that matters most—one that no prizewinning building fully captures.

That strand is people. For me, that's where passion and purpose come together.

I'm so grateful that my working career has brought me opportunities to go all in with my passion to inspire, impress, and improve communities. But the more

People...for me, that's where passion and purpose come together.

healing I experience on my journey, the more I realize that as much as I love to imagine, then realize stunning new buildings, what I most want is to help men to imagine, then realize everything a loving God intends for them.

It's why I have mentored students, leaders, and businessmen over the years.

It's why I wanted to learn from brilliant teachers like Bill Bright, whose lifelong vision was to change every nation on earth, one heart at a time.

It's how ALL IN was born.

It's how this book got written.

Friend, what drives you at your core? What do you want, *really?*

As we have surveyed men in our retreats and forums, the most frequent word they use to describe their journey is *freedom*. Which is exactly as it should be. After all, the apostle Paul declared, "It is for freedom that Christ has set us free."

What an outrageous, wide-open, world-shaking promise!

So let me ask: When you look around your life, your story, your light and dark—do you notice a larger purpose that expresses you more fully rising to the surface? And do you feel freedom in your inner being to pursue it with gusto?

> "It is for freedom that Christ has set us free." What an outrageous, wide-open, world-shaking promise!

Look closely and with a full heart of acceptance for your own story. Because for each of us, our mission is already written on our lives for everyone to read.

I believe our journey inevitably also connects us to what God is doing in our world and what our small but indispensable role in that truly great venture can be.

Our part is to make sure the path we choose is the most exciting and deeply true undertaking we can imagine— then *risk it all for everything that matters*.

That is the deep life journey of a superior man.

pause to reflect

1. In your own words, describe what "the life of the superior man" might look like in your life.

2. What are you willing to *commit* and *do* to become that man?

3. Write down or express to a close friend what is your life passion. Write down or express to a close friend what is your life purpose.

For more free resources, see

how to go all in with god

*I*OPENED THIS BOOK WITH THE STORY OF A CONVERSA-
tion with my friend and mentor Bill Bright. He devoted
his life to taking the good news of freedom in Jesus Christ
around the world.

The good news, Bill said, was life-changing but not
complicated. The way to know God intimately is to take
a leap of faith based on what you know now. Bill put it
this way:

Commit all that you know of yourself
to all that you know of God.

Choosing to go all in with God has brought personal
renewal at the deepest level for millions of people.

What about you?

In the Judeo-Christian tradition, the journey into the inner self brings us more than emotional healing; it also moves us toward a spiritual awakening to God's power and intimate presence in our lives.

If you feel that you have yet to experience that kind of awakening, and want to move toward God in faith, I invite you to take the leap of faith Bill spoke about.

Follow along as I distill four understandings from *All In* that can help you know God more personally as friend and healer.

1. God desires our healing and freedom.

We begin with what we know about God. God loves us and wants us to be free and healed from the painful wounds of our past. We see this promise of redemption often in Scripture.

"It is for freedom that Christ has set us free. Stand firm, then, and do not let yourselves be burdened again by a yoke of slavery" (Galatians 5:1).

"He does not willingly bring affliction or grief to anyone" (Lamentations 3:33).

"He heals the brokenhearted and binds up their wounds" (Psalm 147:3).

Next, what do we now know about ourselves?

2. We all experience hurt, loss, and trauma.

We have blind spots. We struggle to see the truth God wants us to see about ourselves. King David prayed, "I am poor and needy, and my heart is wounded within me" (Psalm 109:22). We carry our pain, and wounds, and hurtful feelings in our hidden inner life. In this book, we have described that hidden blind spot as our "shadow" because it is hard for us to see.

Anger, resentments, and fears flow from these inner wounds, which often stem from painful injuries or messages we received in childhood. We often express this pain in addictions, rage, and dysfunctional behavior to compensate for our pain. In our blindness, we may hurt ourselves and others and may feel far from God.

3. The need for spiritual healing and the light of truth is universal.

Jesus said, "Your eye is the lamp of your body. When your eyes are healthy, your whole body also is full of light. But when they are unhealthy, your body also is full of darkness" (Luke 11:34).

There is a way out. We can bring our great need into the light of truth. God's Spirit will lead the way.

"I, the LORD ... will take hold of your hand. I will keep you and will make you to be a covenant for the people and a light ... to open eyes that are blind, to free captives from prison and to release from the dungeon those who sit in darkness" (Isaiah 42:6–7).

"He reveals deep and hidden things; he knows what lies in darkness, and light dwells with him" (Daniel 2:22).

"Come to me, all you who are weary and burdened, and I will give you rest" (Jesus, in Matthew 11:28).

il #5

Shining Light into Our Shadow
The Hidden Power of Our Shadow

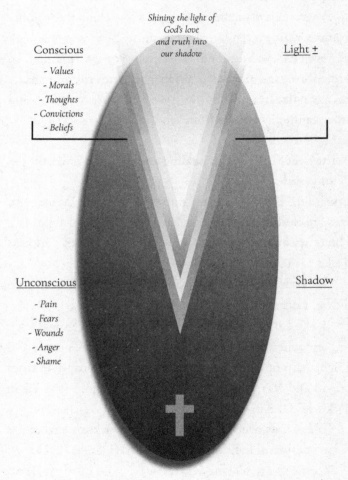

*Shining the light of
God's love
and truth into
our shadow*

<u>Conscious</u>

- Values
- Morals
- Thoughts
- Convictions
- Beliefs

<u>Light ±</u>

<u>Unconscious</u>

- Pain
- Fears
- Wounds
- Anger
- Shame

<u>Shadow</u>

God is comfortable in our shadow:
accepting, loving, and waiting for us there

4. The deeper we go into our shadow to see the truth about ourselves, the more we will find that God is already there with his unlimited love, acceptance, and forgiveness.

The following illustration shows you what I mean: God *wants* to show us the hidden truth within us! King David wrote, "Behold, You desire truth in the innermost being, and in the hidden part You will make me know wisdom" (Psalm 51:6 NASB1995).

Once we embrace the truth about us, we can receive God's gifts of forgiveness, healing, and freedom.

As we bring our inner truth into the light, a cleansing healing begins.

"Create in me a clean heart, O God, and renew a steadfast spirit within me" (Psalm 51:10 NASB1995).

"The sacrifices of God are a broken spirit; a broken and a contrite heart, O God, You will not despise" (Psalm 51:17 NASB1995).

As we open ourselves to see more of the truth about ourselves, we can receive spiritual and emotional renewal. Jesus said, "[If] they would see with their eyes, hear with their ears, and understand with their heart and return ... I would heal them" (Matthew 13:15 NASB1995).

The apostle Paul wrote, "For he has rescued us from the dominion of darkness and brought us into the kingdom of the Son he loves, in whom we have redemption, the forgiveness of sins" (Colossians 1:13–14).

your personal leap of faith

I've worked through these powerful understandings with scores of men, in one-on-one conversation and in groups. If you have sensed a heart response as I've unfolded these key insights, I encourage you to make your personal leap of faith.

As you have learned by now, men flourish best in the company of like-minded men, so I encourage you to invite a wise friend or counselor to work through this commitment with you. "The purposes of a person's heart are deep waters, but one who has insight draws them out" (Proverbs 20:5). **But whether you're with a friend or alone, your leap of faith begins with a prayer.**

Prayer is simply an honest conversation with God. Your prayer now might follow this time-honored path.

First, humbly ask God to show you the truth that he wants you to see.

Then, ask him to forgive you for the hurt you have caused others and ask for forgiveness for those who have hurt you.

Finally, ask him to begin to heal the wounds in your shadow and set you free.

a journey of beginning

This is not the end of the journey but the beginning. As I suggested earlier, a man's journey inward can feel like peeling an onion: we come to awareness about one important truth only to discover that many more layers of truth await.

So the journey we're talking about is ongoing. Which is why we can all benefit from journeying together with a skilled counselor or other honest, confidential friends who are courageous enough to honestly seek the truth about themselves.

God is with us on this journey—and he is *not* a neutral observer. God *wants* to reveal deeper truth to those who seek him!

Through the process, Christ gives us his Holy Spirit as our Comforter and Counselor (John 14:26) as he guides us into all truth (John 16:13). And he gives us one another (Romans 12:5) in a healing, redeeming community where the truth is spoken in love (Ephesians 4:15).

Together, as we read and apply the Bible and fellowship with Jesus, our journey of spiritual growth promises joy and wholeness, both in ourselves and in our relationships with others.

For more free resources, see

glossary

addiction. A simple definition I find useful is, "Anything that hurts us or those we love that we keep on doing anyway." People with addiction use substances (such as alcohol or other drugs) or engage in behaviors (such as gambling or sex) that become compulsive and often continue despite harmful consequences.

Al-Anon. Al-Anon is a mutual-support program for those whose lives have been affected by someone else's drinking (or drugging). By sharing common experiences and applying the Al-Anon principles, families and friends of alcoholics can bring positive changes to their individual situations, whether or not the alcoholic admits the existence of a drinking problem or seeks help.

Alcoholics Anonymous. Alcoholics Anonymous is an international fellowship of men and women who have had a drinking problem. In AA meetings, men and women share their experiences, strength, and hope with one another that they may solve their common problem and help others to recover from alcoholism. The only requirement for membership is a desire to stop drinking. AA's Twelve Steps—which are the inspiration for most twelve-step recovery programs—are a group of principles, spiritual in nature, which, if practiced as a way of life, can relieve a sufferer's obsession with alcohol and enable him or her to recover a happy, useful life.

boundaries. Henry Cloud and John Townsend, in their book *Boundaries*, explain the term thus: "Any confusion of responsibility and ownership in our lives is a problem of boundaries. Just as homeowners set physical boundary lines around their land, we need to set mental, physical, emotional, and spiritual boundaries around our lives to help us distinguish what is our responsibility and what isn't."

circle of grace. In this book, a circle of grace describes the experience of a group in which people experience confidential, honest, deeply respectful relationships; they are invited to share their stories, knowing that they will be received gently, in a relationship of caring, mercy, and rigorous commitment to their well-being and future growth. On page 38, we describe it as "a circle of like-minded men, each broken in different places, who take risks to share their deepest truths, listen well, and stand alongside one another in solidarity, believing heart and soul in one another's worth."

codependent. Codependency is a behavioral condition in a relationship where one person enables another person's addiction, poor mental health, immaturity, irresponsibility, or underachievement. Among the core characteristics of codependency is an excessive reliance on other people for approval and a sense of identity.

codependent "death spiral." A destructive codependent relationship, where each person triggers and reinforces the increasingly destructive conflict.

dysfunctional. A synonym for "broken" that describes individuals, relationships, and environments (such as home, work, church) where assumptions and patterns of behavior are unhealthy, manipulative, and often destructive.

father wound. An injury to the psyche usually received in childhood that damages a person's core sense of self and shapes his feelings and behaviors in unhealthy ways. For example, a father wound can negatively influence a person's experience in adulthood of self-worth, confidence, safety from male anger or violence, and purpose.

grace. The word translated *grace* in the New Testament comes from the Greek word *charis*, which means "favor, blessing, or kindness." In Christian theology, grace is the help given to us by God because God *of his own nature* desires us to have it, not necessarily because of anything we have done to earn it. It is understood to be a spontaneous gift from God to people—generous, free, and totally unexpected and undeserved—that takes the form of divine blessing, love, forgiveness, and a share in the divine life of God. By giving and receiving grace in relationships, we demonstrate the divine nature and ultimate generosity to others.

mother wound. Injury to the psyche usually received in childhood that damages a person's core sense of self and shapes their feelings and behaviors in unhealthy ways. For example, a mother wound can negatively influence a person's experience in adulthood of bonding, security and trust, and self-worth.

passion. In this book, I use the word to mean a powerful, unique conviction or drive at the core of a man's being that gives him a special sense of calling and the intense desire to pursue it with gusto.

persona. A persona is a false but preferred self that a person wants to show to the world. It is a role or facade that an individual chooses over their authentic self. Jung called it "a kind of mask, designed on the one hand to make a definite impression upon others, and on the other to conceal the true nature of the individual."

primal wound. A formative disruption or violation that leaves a child feeling that the original connection to the parent is threatened or has been cut off. The injury may become a person's motivating force—sometimes expressed defensively (as in, the one thing we strive to prove is *not* true about us). It may result in a broken relationship with a parent, others, and the world. In psychological terms, our connection to our deeper self is wounded.

projection. *Psychology Today* defines projection as "the process of displacing one's feelings onto a different person, animal, or object. The term is most commonly used to describe defensive projection—attributing one's own unacceptable urges to another. For example, if someone continuously bullies and ridicules a peer about his insecurities, the bully might be projecting his own struggle with self-esteem onto the other person."

purpose. In this book, we say that passion and purpose are inextricably linked. If our passion is the unique, intense desire that drives us, then purpose is what gives our passion direction.

shadow. The *shadow* is a word introduced by Carl Jung to describe the dark, hidden, or unseen side of someone's personality. The shadow describes an unconscious aspect of the personality that the conscious ego does not identify in itself, or the entirety of the unconscious—i.e., everything of which a person is not fully conscious. The unknown or hidden part of our self. In Jungian thought, the shadow can include everything outside the light of consciousness and may be positive or negative. Because one tends to reject or remain ignorant of the least desirable aspects of one's personality, the shadow is largely negative. There are, however, positive aspects that may also remain hidden in one's shadow (especially in people with low self-esteem, anxieties, and false beliefs).

shadow work. Shadow work refers to the therapeutic process that helps a person get in touch with the unknown or hidden parts of the self that have been overlooked or repressed. The unconscious plays a large role in shaping our thoughts, emotions, and behaviors. The goal of shadow work is to make those unconscious fixations—such as the pain of a traumatic event—part of your conscious awareness so that you can then work on them in therapy. In this book we use language of light and dark to visualize the conscious and unconscious parts of our self. The dark parts are the source of impulsive, often unwanted, and unreasonable parts of ourselves, but "shadow" does not equal "bad": our dark side can be the source of passion, creativity, and insight.

success and achievement addiction. Like any other addiction, success and achievement addiction (or workaholism) describes an inability to stop a behavior that may bring some reward but also serious negative consequences. It often stems from a compulsive need to achieve status and success or to escape emotional stress. Work addiction is common in people described as ambitious, goal-oriented perfectionists. Much like someone with a drug addiction, a person with a success or achievement addiction may be unable to stop the behavior even when its negative impacts on their relationships or physical or mental health become apparent.

triggers. A trigger in psychology is a stimulus such as a smell, sound, or sight that generates feelings of trauma. People typically use this term when describing post-traumatic stress (PTSD).

wounds. A formative injury to the emotional or spiritual part of a person, usually from abuse, abandonment, or neglect. The language of wounding is helpful because it suggests that if a person can bring loving attention to the source of pain, and the narrative around it, healing and recovery is possible.

reading guide
FOR INDIVIDUAL REFLECTION
AND GROUP DISCUSSION

I'M ALWAYS AMAZED AT HOW MUCH MORE A BOOK means to me when I take the time to write down how it applies to me personally or talk it through with friends. That's what I hope this reading guide to *All In* can facilitate for you. I recommend you engage with the questions first on your own in a time of focused reflection and journaling. Then get together with other men on the same journey to share your thoughts and listen to what they have to say.

I promise you'll make important discoveries about yourself, your life story, your feelings, and your current challenges. In fact, consider using this book to start your own ALL IN group. (For more resources in this regard, go to www.allinbook.com.) You'll be making a life-changing investment in yourself and all those who journey with you. It certainly has been that for me.

—*Allen*

(*A note: While all questions lend themselves to conversation, three in each chapter are particularly well suited for sharing and exploring with others. These have been marked with the discussion icon* ⬚ .)

chapter 1: the view from the top

1. Not far into his opening chapter, Allen puts his offer on the table: "This is a book for men who are ready to explore the terra incognita [unknown territory] of their hidden self in order to achieve the life they deeply want." Reading those words made you feel (choose one):

   a. Excited and lucky—"Let's go! This is going to be great!"

   b. Open, but cautious—"Okay, but one step at a time and we'll see where this goes."

   c. Relieved—"Finally. This might be just what I've been waiting for."

   d. Nervous—"Um, my 'hidden self'? I'm pretty sure it's a snake pit in there!"

2. Have you gone through a "my little kingdom is crumbling" moment? If so, what precipitated the crisis for you? What did you most fear losing? ⬚

3. Do you agree with Allen's observation, "The very same skills, values, and mindset that catapult you up in life can also bring you crashing down"? ⬚

4. Beginning with "We crave freedom yet ..." on page 31, Allen identifies paradoxes that most men can relate to. Of the four listed, which one describes you best? Why?

5. If you have been in a group of men where you felt a strong sense of being both known and fully accepted, what was that like? What did the experience show you? 💬

chapter 2: something isn't working

1. Allen's headaches seemed to come out of nowhere, but at the time, he was facing significant challenges personally and professionally. Can you relate to health issues that most likely were connected to extreme circumstances you were facing? 💬

2. When Allen slows down to take a good, hard look, he's stunned to realize that his company is broken, starting at the top. Imagine you're Allen's friend, and you're meeting with him over coffee. How would you want to be a friend in that situation? If the moment was right, what encouraging story from your own life could you share with him? 💬

3. Pain drove Allen to consider stepping away from the very career he'd given his life to. Have you ever walked away from a job or something in your life that you felt defined you? How did you feel doing so? 💬

4. Competitive, goal-oriented guys famously don't know when to quit—whether at the end of the day, or the week, or in the grip of a health crisis. Would you say this is true, or mostly true, for you? If yes, how has that affected you?

5. Allen determined he needed a sabbatical to get to the bottom of what was going on in his life. While you may not have the ability to call a full time-out, would you consider setting time aside in your life with the specific purpose of gaining clarity? What might that look like?

chapter 3: waking up to what's inside

1. In your family of origin, how were you taught to relate to
   your feelings? What was modeled to you? 🗨

2. A group facilitator pressed Allen to notice the inconsistencies between *what he said he wanted* and *what he actually did*.
   Have you seen this disconnect playing out in your life? If
   so, how?

3. Like many men, Allen found it hard to connect with his
   feelings. But he learned there was tremendous value in
   doing so. Would you say you (a) more often feel scared or
   (b) more often feel angry? How does that emotion show up
   in your actions and relationships?

4. Allen tells the story of the annual Christmas party, when
   his daughter is upstairs seriously ill. Allen and his wife
   are downstairs busy hosting. Allen decides to delegate his
   daughter's care to a friend who is a nurse, checking on her
   only when the party is over. What were you thinking and
   feeling while Allen was telling this story? Have you ever
   been so disconnected from your primary relationships that
   you failed to understand the seriousness of a circumstance?
   Why do you think that was the case? 🗨

5. Allen encounters what he calls a "circle of grace" at an AA
   meeting. He describes it as "a loving, honest, compassionate
   and empathetic community. No judgment, criticism, or
   how-to-fix-it advice. Just broken people like me sharing
   honestly about their struggles." Have you ever experienced
   what Allen describes? If not, what would you be willing to
   risk to experience it? 🗨

chapter 4: troubling revelations

1. Codependence can be a difficult behavior to understand—
   and even more difficult to recognize in ourselves. Have you
   ever felt you were working harder on a friend's or family
   member's issues than they were? Describe what that looked
   like and how you felt about your choices. 🗫

2. How much of your impulse to help others would you say
   comes from your need for affirmation or praise?

3. Allen defines addictions as "anything that hurts us or those
   we love that we keep on doing anyway." Leaving aside
   substances for the moment, where do you see addictive
   behavior or tendencies in your life? 🗫

4. Allen draws a direct link between repeated sacrifices for
   another person and the emotion of resentment. How would
   you rate your familiarity with resentment?
   a. "Ridiculously familiar. Seems like it's my go-to poison."
   b. "Very familiar at times in my life."
   c. "Not very familiar. I don't think I am all that vulnerable
      to resentment."
   d. "Not familiar at all. I make a point of not keeping a
      ledger on how people treat me."

5. You, your wife, your family all benefit from your hard work.
   You, your wife, your family also all think you work too
   hard and long. What's a guy to do? What are ways that
   you try to resolve the conflict? And how is that working
   for you? 🗫

chapter 5: crashing into the past

1. In this chapter, Allen reaches back to tell his family story, going back to his Grandpa Jack. What he sees is an incredible drive to succeed that was originally fueled by hunger and want. He concludes, "We could almost say our past writes our present." What did your family of origin teach you, directly or indirectly, about dealing with anger? About dealing with fear? How do you see your past playing out in your story now?

2. He writes, "Emotional injury becomes an inheritance passed down intentionally or unintentionally—and often both—from father, to son, to grandson." Are you aware of a wound or wounds that you have inherited from your father? 🗨

3. Later in the chapter, Allen identifies "I am not enough" as one of his inherited messages. Can you identify messages handed down to you? How have they shaped / how are they shaping your career and relationships? 🗨

4. Allen tells the story of crashing in an aircraft he was piloting while flying friends to a wedding. The story starts out as a rollicking adventure tale of a brave young pilot. But by the end of the chapter—and with the passage of time—other meanings surface. What are they?

5. As you reflect on your life story, what emotions or themes do you see running through it? Has the meaning of a significant event in your life shifted with time and perspective? If so, how? 🗨

chapter 6: journey into the shadow

1. Our shadow self, Jung said, describes the part of our subconscious mind where we hide away taboo or unwanted thoughts, memories, feelings, and desires. What was your initial reaction to the thought that this might be true for you? 🗨

2. Have you tended to view your conscious beliefs, convictions, and commitments as what really defines you? If so, where would you say that life outlook came from?

3. Allen describes how our shadow plays a role in helping us initially cope with early childhood wounds that we didn't have the capacity to process at the time. If left alone and not brought to light, those unhealed places can have significant impact on how we behave in our current everyday lives. Can you think of childhood circumstances that might have played a role in unwanted behaviors you're experiencing today? 🗨

4. Allen writes, "In the light of awareness and acceptance, the shadow loses power to do harm." What might your life look like if the shadow began losing power?

5. According to Kimberly Fosu, "We lash out at people for the behaviors we don't like in ourselves." Agree or disagree? Explain. 🗨

chapter 7: when good men fall

1. Allen writes that for leaders around midlife, the weight of their unexamined shadow can become unbearable. He uses the image of a beach ball bursting to the surface to describe how life events that have been repressed or kept secret can suddenly burst into the open, causing great damage. In what ways have you seen this dynamic play out in your life? 🗩

2. About leaders, Allen says, "Because we live in the spotlight, we go to extremes to protect our public image. Which isn't us, of course—it's just our persona or social face we present to the world." How would an observer describe your public persona? How do you protect your public image? How might your persona be negatively affecting you personally? 🗩

3. Allen shares how painful it was for him when the double life of a longtime friend and Christian leader came to light. Where have you experienced betrayal? Describe what that felt like. Can you identify a time when someone may have felt you were the betrayer? If so, how did that make you feel?

4. Look again at Allen's retelling of the film *Chocolat*, page 131. Describe a time when you were outed for compromising behavior. Did you encounter a grace-filled friend who accepted your humanity and helped you recover?

5. In this chapter, Allen shares five questions he wrestled with. As he explores the fourth question, he offers two kinds of transparency that can help us stay off the "burned list." Explain each. Which of the two most reflects your life right now? 🗩

chapter 8: breaking free from toxic emotions

1. Keeping things real, Allen opens the chapter with painful admissions surrounding the disintegration of his first marriage. Which part of his account evoked the strongest reaction in you, and why?

2. He concludes, "If we fail to make that connection between old wounds and intense emotion now, these powerful feelings can drive our lives in ways we will come to regret." What powerful feelings have you had in the past six months that might be connected to old wounds, perhaps from your childhood? How did the wounds happen, and what was the recent impact? 🗨

3. Consider the combat and revenge movies that boys and men typically enjoy. Why do you think acting out in anger and violence—even just watching it on the screen—can feel so satisfying to a guy? 🗨

4. Allen identifies shame as one of four powerful negative emotions for men. Where do you think most of us initially learned to feel shame? Do you think guys who grow up in church are especially susceptible to shame? Give examples to support your view. 🗨

5. Allen admits that letting go of resentments and anger surrounding the breakup of his first marriage was not a onetime thing but a process of him letting go—only to reach for the grievance again. Can you relate? What has helped you the most to keep moving toward reconciliation and acceptance?

chapter 9: circle of trust

1. Let's say you're invited to attend the kind of men's group discussed in this chapter. The friend inviting you says, "It's so great. We really get honest." How are you most likely to feel when you first get the invitation? After sleeping on it? After you talk it over with your wife? 🗩

2. Allen says, "A man who's committed to reaching peak performance is most likely to achieve it in the company of others striving for the same goal." What do you say? What do you think the benefits might be of sharing your journey with other men and being let into theirs as well?

3. Good leaders pay close attention to group dynamics. Have you paid close attention to the persona you convey in a group? If someone else described your persona in a group (one you're not leading), what would they likely say? Have you asked a colleague to do that for you? 🗩

4. For a group to be purposefully transformational, Allen says, it must "regularly affirm our mutual guarantee of confidentiality." Have you ever experienced the kind of absolute trust in a small group that allows for each member to be truly authentic? If so, what was the impact of that experience?

5. In your own words, describe the process of a clearing. In a situation where a group member is feeling bruised and disrespected, what benefits would you expect from using such a process? What risks? What value would you expect if you applied the general principles of clearing in your everyday life? 🗩

chapter 10: everything that matters

1. Allen writes, "The goal of this book has been to motivate you to do the hard work of uncovering your true self: of looking deep inside for clues to what drives us—and sometimes drives us wrong." In just a few words, describe what you've realized about your true self that you didn't know before. 💬

2. As a result of your new insight, is there something in your life that you hope is possible now that didn't seem so before? What might that look like if you were to pursue it? 💬

3. Allen writes, "My power is greatest when I am directly connected to my passion." When you sense you are losing the joy of your "original fire," what do you do to regain it?

4. As Allen acknowledges, most men struggle at times to identify why we're on earth. How do you define your purpose? Is your purpose directly connected to your passion? When you think of your passion, do you think first of your work life or do you connect it more to other parts of your life? If both, do you see a connection between them?

5. Allen realizes that living for people is where his passion and purpose come together. Where would you say your passion and purpose come together? What does (or could) that feel like for you? What are some outcomes that you could visualize? Could that be your life mission? 💬

For additional free resources, see www.allinbook.com.

notes

1   The May 2021 American Perspectives Survey found that, in spite of the pervasiveness of social media, Americans report having fewer close friendships. Men have been hit the hardest. Thirty years ago, their 1990 study showed that 55% of men reported having at least six close friends. Today, that number has been cut in half. Only 27% of men report having at least six or more close friends, and 15% have no close friendships at all.

2   In his book *The Masculine Journey* (1993), Robert Hicks offers an expanded list of what men want. He cites clinical psychologist John Friel, who believed that men want seven things: to feel more, to befriend more, to learn to love, to find meaningful work, to father significantly, to be whole, and to heal and reconcile. Hicks concludes, "Each man wants a greater unity to his life that allows him more freedom to feel, enjoy, praise, reconcile, and see meaning in his important relationships" (p. 126).

3   Ecclesiastes 4:8.

4   For further reading, see Allan N. Schore, *The Development of the Unconscious Mind* (New York: W. W. Norton & Company, 2019); Allan N. Schore, "The Right Brain Implicit Self Lies at the Core of Psychoanalysis," *Psychoanalytic Dialogues* 21 (2011): 75–100; and Bruce Ecker, Robin Ticic, and Laurel Hulley, *Unlocking the Emotional Brain* (New York: Routledge, 2012).

5   See Efrat Ginot, *The Neuropsychology of the Unconscious: Integrating Brain and Mind in Psychotherapy* (New York: W. W. Norton & Company, 2015).

6   C. G. Jung, Gerhard Adler ed., trans., et al., *Collected Works of C. G. Jung*, volume 9 (part 2), *Aion: Researches into the Phenomenology of the Self*, 2nd rev. ed. , Kindle Edition (Princeton University Press, 2014).

7   For further study, Dr. John Townsend recommends these supporting sources: Natalie Beck, "Beginning with the Body: The Neurobiology of Mind-

fulness," in *Cultivating Mindfulness in Clinical Social Work: Narratives from Practice,* ed. Terry B. Northcut (Chicago: Springer, 2017); Alan Fogel, *Body Sense: The Science and Practice of Embodied Self-Awareness* (New York: W. W. Norton, 2013); and Alan Fogel, *The Psychophysiology of Self-Awareness: Rediscovering the Lost Art of Body Sense* (New York: W. W. Norton, 2009).

8 For excellent general references regarding Jung's concept of the shadow, see Allan Kaplan, *Development Practitioners and Social Process: Artists of the Invisible* (London: Pluto Press, 2002); and John P. Conger, *Jung & Reich: The Body as Shadow,* 2nd ed. (Berkely, CA: North Atlantic Books, 2005).

9 Proverbs 4:23.

10 C. G. Jung, Aniela Jaffe ed., Richard Winston and Clara Winston trans., *Memories, Dreams, Reflections* (New York: Pantheon, 1963), 247.

11 C. S. Lewis, *The Problem of Pain* (HarperCollins, 2001), 88–89.

12 Danny Silk, Facebook post, https://www.facebook.com/permalink. php?id=121990546910&story_fbid=10151578471001911.

13 "What Is Codependency?," LaJolla Recovery, September 27, 2019, https://lajollarecovery.com/2019/09/what-is-codependency/.

14 Russ Rainey, "Codependency: What Is It?," Focus on the Family, July 17, 2017, https://www.focusonthefamily.com/get-help/codependency-what-is-it/.

15 Pia Mellody, *Facing Codependence: What It Is, Where It Comes from, How It Sabotages Our Lives* (New York: Harper & Row, 2003).

16 Henry Cloud and John Townsend, *Boundaries: When to Say Yes, How to Say No to Take Control of Your Life* (Grand Rapids, MI: Zondervan, 1992).

17 Arthur C. Brooks, "'Success Addicts' Choose Being Special over Being Happy," *Atlantic,* July 30, 2020, https://www.theatlantic.com/family/archive/2020/07/why-success-wont-make-you-happy/614731/.

18 William James, *Psychology* (New York: Henry Holt, 1905), 179.

19 John Eldredge, *Wild at Heart Field Guide:* rev. ed. (New York: Thomas Nelson, 2021), 90.

20 Richard Rohr, "Unveiling the Shadow," June 13, 2021, Center for Action and Contemplation, https://cac.org/unveiling-the-shadow-2021-06-13/.

21 Romans 7:22–23.

22 Matthew 6:22–23.

23 All notes for Fosu are from her article "Shadow Work: A Simple Guide to Transcending the Darker Aspects of the Self," *Medium,* November 24, 2020,

https://medium.com/big-self-society/shadow-work-a-simple-guide-to-transcending-the-darker-aspects-of-the-self-e948ee285723.

24 Ephesians 3:16–18; italics mine.

25 "The Persona: Archetype Anatomy," Envision Your Evolution, June 11, 2019, https://www.envisionyourevolution.com/analytical-psychology/persona-archetype-anatomy/157/.

26 Richard Rohr, "Living the Shadow," June 15, 2021, Center for Action and Contemplation, https://cac.org/living-the-shadow-2021-06-15/.

27 Rick Warren, author of The Purpose Driven Life, @RickWarren, "RATIO-NALIZE = to tell yourself rational lies," December 3, 2009, 3:26 PM, https://twitter.com/rickwarren/status/6315557546?lang=en.

28 Jeremiah 17:9 NKJV.

29 Romans 3:23 NKJV.

30 James 3:1.

31 Richard Rohr, "Shadow Work: A Necessary Negativity," Center for Action and Contemplation, June 18, 2021, https://cac.org/a-necessary-negativity-2021-06-18/.

32 James 5:16; italics mine.

33 Psalm 51:6 NASB1995.

34 Proverbs 24:16 NASB1995.

35 Henry Nouwen, "The Wounded Healer," Henry Nouwen Society, https://henrinouwen.org/meditation/the-wounded-healer/.

36 Deuteronomy 32:35; Romans 12:19 NASB1995.

37 Joseph Campbell, The Hero with a Thousand Faces (Novato, CA: New World Library, 2008).

38 "Imago Relationship Therapy," Quantum Love, https://www.quantumlove.com/imago-relationship-therapy.html.

39 Ecclesiastes 4:9–10, 12.

40 Shirzad Chamine, Positive Intelligence: Why Only 20% of Teams and Individuals Achieve Their True Potential and How You Can Achieve Yours (Austin: Greenleaf Book Group Press, 2012).

41 Shirzad Chamine, Positive Intelligence.

42 For their excellent resource for leaders of small groups in a church setting, see Henry Cloud and John Townsend, Making Small Groups Work (Grand Rapids, MI: Zondervan, 2003).

43 David Deida, The Way of the Superior Man: A Spiritual Guide to Mastering

the Challenges of Women, Work, and Sexual Desire, rev. ed. (Boulder, CO: Sounds True, 2017), 36.

44 Brené Brown, online at Brenebrown.com, and in *Rising Strong: How the Ability to Reset Transforms the Way We Live, Love, Parent, and Lead* (New York:Spiegel & Grau, 2015).

45 David Deida, *The Way of the Superior Man: A Spiritual Guide to Mastering the Challenges of Women, Work, and Sexual Desire*, rev. ed. (Boulder, CO: Sounds True, 2017).

46 See note 2 for an expanded list of what men want according to Robert Hicks in *The Masculine Journey*, 126.

47 Kate Miller, "Do the Math: Taking a Look at Our Impact in the Workplace," Preaching.com, https://www.preaching.com/leadership/do-the-math-taking-a-look-at-our-impact-in-the-workplace/.

48 Frederick Buechner, "Vocation," Frederick Buechner Center, July 18, 2017, https://www.frederickbuechner.com/quote-of-the-day/2017/7/18/vocation.

49 Galatians 5:1.

about the
author

W. ALLEN MORRIS,
CHAIRMAN AND CEO OF THE
ALLEN MORRIS COMPANY

A LLEN MORRIS IS CHAIRMAN AND CEO OF THE ALLEN
Morris Company in Coral Gables, Florida. He is a
leading authority on real estate topics and has appeared
frequently on the Fox Business news show *Cavuto* with
Neil Cavuto, and on *Fox Business Morning Break* with
Charles Payne. He has written numerous real estate arti-
cles, including for a monthly blog, *Allen Morris on Real
Estate*, and is the author of the book *A Critical Look at
Jesus: A Skeptic's Approach*.

The Allen Morris Company, now in its sixty-third year
and with over eighty-five successful developments to its
credit, is one of the largest developers of office, multifamily,

condominium, hotel, and mixed-use projects in Florida and Georgia. The company is headquartered in the Mediterranean Revival–style Alhambra Towers, located in downtown Coral Gables, Florida. Alhambra Towers has won ten awards.

Two recent major award-winning projects include the SLS LUX Brickell, a 1.4-million-square-foot, $350 million, fifty-eight-story luxury hotel and condominium in Miami (a joint venture with Related Group); and the $71 million Maitland City Centre, which created a new mixed-use Live-Work-Play downtown for the City of Maitland, Florida. The company's Hermitage Apartment Homes, St. Petersburg, and the SLS LUX Brickell are both recipients of the Florida's Best Award.

In 2020, the Allen Morris Company completed their eighty-third project: the Julian, a 409-unit apartment residence in Creative Village, an urban innovation district in downtown Orlando. In 2021, the company completed their eighty-fourth project, the 409-unit Star Metals Residences in Atlanta, and also their eighty-fifth project, the 267,000-square-foot Star Metals Offices in Atlanta, with the Star Metals Hotel coming soon.

In addition to being an officer and director of more than one hundred different real estate related companies, Allen Morris is president of a charitable foundation and art museum. He is a graduate of the Georgia Institute of Technology and Harvard Business School and is pursuing postgraduate studies at Oxford University. He holds the professional real estate designations of CCIM, SIOR, CPM, CRE, and FRICS.

Allen has been an active member of the Young Presidents Organization (YPO) since 1982. He is the former chairman of the Florida YPO chapter and is currently a member of YPO Gold Chapter and board member of the Greater Miami Chamber of Commerce and the United Way of Miami-Dade County. He has served as chairman of the VeritageMiami Wine and Food Festival and is a lifetime senior member of the Orange Bowl Committee. He has served on many national and local real estate boards and many local philanthropic boards.

He has received numerous professional distinctions, including the 2014 Business Leader of the Year from the Coral Gables Chamber of Commerce and the 2016 Miami-Dade County Chairman of the Year Apogee Award from *South Florida Business and Wealth* magazine; he was selected as a 2017 Power Leader in Real Estate by the *South Florida Business Journal* and, most recently, granted the 2019 Lifetime Achievement Award of the Greater Miami Chamber of Commerce. He is a recipient of the Institute of Human Relations Award given by the American Jewish Committee and the prestigious Hickok Award from the Young Presidents Organization.

Allen's mission and the mission of his company is to "Inspire, Impress, and Improve" the lives of everyone they touch. His favorite saying sits on the edge of his desk facing visitors: "How CAN it be done?"

In his personal life, Allen is a commercial-rated jet pilot and a fourth-degree black belt Tae Kwon Do Master, and he enjoys scuba diving, hunting, and world travel. He is married to June Morris and has four adult children, two stepdaughters, and three grandchildren.

For more information, visit www.allinbook.com.